What's Wrong with Labour?

A critical history of the Labour Party
in the twentieth century

Paul Allender

MERLIN PRESS

First published 2001
by The Merlin Press Ltd.
PO Box 30705
London
WC2E 8QD

© Paul Allender 2001

The author asserts the moral right to be identified as the author of this work

British Library Cataloguing in Publication Data is available from the
British Library

ISBN: 0-85036-497-3

Typeset by Jon Carpenter

Printed in the UK

Contents

Acknowledgements

I would like to thank my family Helen and Georgie for their love and psychological support. I simply could not have done it without them.

Next, my mum and dad for being there. My dad for lots of telephone conversations about the current progress of Sheffield Wednesday and both of them for providing me with information regarding particular aspects of Sheffield's labour movement.

My friends and colleagues in Canterbury, particularly Alison Edgley, David McLellan and Liz Mitchell.

David Coates for years of support and political and intellectual inspiration.

Anne O'Daly for constant support, encouragement, love, audio tapes and tickets to see *Forced Entertainment*.

As regards the Sheffield case study, all of the interviewees but particularly Pat Heath, Alan Wigfield, Dan Sequerra and Ted Thorne for their support. Also Ahmed Gurnah and Chris Croome for providing me with contacts.

Julia Twigg and Andrew Fenyo at the University of Kent for advice and assistance.

Last, but certainly not least, Sheffield Wednesday FC, particularly Chris Waddle and Des Walker, for providing inspiration and hope (and occasional despair!). You were always on my mind.

Foreword

This book could not be more timely. It is a critique, from the independent left, of the goals and methods espoused by the Labour Party during the one hundred years which have just elapsed since its foundation. Many would agree with Paul Allender that the record of the Labour Party during the last century has largely been one of failure, both electorally and in terms of achieved social reform: Labour has failed to provide decent living standards for the majority of its natural supporters and fallen well short of fulfilling the hopes and aspirations at the core of the socialist movement. Most are inclined to see this process as a gradual abandonment of positive socialist principles, whether due to the cynicism inherent in the Actonian dictum about power and corruption or to a more sociological approach about the conservatism of mass movements following Michels. But Allender presents us with a refreshingly novel perspective: he draws upon academic analysis and extensive practical experience of the Labour movement to give an insightful and original account of the ineffectiveness of the Labour Party.

It is not that the Labour Party has abandoned socialist principles – it never had them in the first place. Through a careful analysis of Labourist theory and practice, Allender shows that the failure of the Labour Party is inherent in the very logic of Labourism. New Labour, in other words, is not that new after all: it is merely the contemporary application of the ideology which has permeated the Labour Party since its inception. The bottles may be new but the wine is old. For all those who wish to think critically about the structure, ideology and practice of the Labour Party, Paul Allender has provided us with a powerful historical and analytical perspective.

David McLellan
Professor of Political Theory, Goldsmiths College

Preface

This book aims to provide a characterization of the British Labour Party for the whole of its existence, since the creation of the Labour Representation Committee in 1900. Almost unavoidably, I am approaching the subject from a critical perspective. That is, I did not set out to write a balanced and would-be objective account of Labour's history.

Why is a critical perspective unavoidable? I was born and grew up in Sheffield, South Yorkshire in a period of economic boom for the city and the heyday of local labourism. I left Sheffield in 1976 but all my family have remained there, and I am still, despite having lived in the South of England for the last twenty-two years, very much a Sheffielder. The Labour Party was the only political party worthy of mention locally as I was growing up and it directly and, perhaps more importantly, indirectly influenced my and my family's lives in many and various ways. These included contributing towards a general co-operative and collective approach to life, plus the more specific social and cultural aspects such as the working-men's clubs, organized collective activities, sports and various outings to the countryside and seaside resorts. The 'culture of labourism', to borrow John Marriott's (1991) term, was ever-present.

Labour has also been very important to me in adult life, in a number of other ways. I was a member of the party from 1980 to 1985 in Putney, South-West London. The first three of these were very definitely 'Bennite' years and I was a very keen and tireless activist working to try to get Peter Hain elected to parliament. This project failed, as did my enthusiasm for the Labour Party. I had further direct experiences of labourism. I worked as an employee for the National Union of Teachers, calculating strike pay. I worked for Islington Council at the time that Margaret Hodge was its leader. It had just decentralized its services and, despite teething troubles, this was generally a positive time. I worked as a researcher for a campaigning housing organization in the London

Borough of Camden which had, at the time, a strong Labour council. Last, but certainly not least, I worked from 1990 to 1996 as a Research Officer for the National Union of Students (NUS), an organization that was dominated by labourist ideas and actions. In fact, it was actually directly dominated by 'Walworth Road', the then Labour Party Headquarters. While at the NUS I gained a lot of experience of working in parliament and campaigning with other national organisations. Additionally, I have been a member of various trade unions, sometimes active and sometimes more of an observer.

All these specific experiences, plus more general ones as a media watcher of the Labour Party in opposition and now in government, have inspired me to read extensively on the subject. To attempt to summarize my feelings about labourism, a deep sense of dissatisfaction and disquiet has pervaded most if not all of the above experiences. I will not dwell on this here as it is the main motivation for the work that follows. It is sufficient for me to state that I have direct personal experience of the Labour Party and movement as well as intellectual experience and knowledge of the subject. It is the former that has informed and motivated the latter.

However, the arguments that follow are not my isolated thoughts on the subject. Since leaving the Labour Party in 1985 I have been a member of some, and have been in contact with other, independent left organizations such as the Socialist Society, the Socialist Movement, the Independent Labour Network, etc. My analysis of labourism has been informed by the thoughts and actions of some of these groups, as well as by key intellectuals such as Ralph Miliband and David Coates. The one person who has been ever-present in these groups and has therefore been the most influential activist on my work is Hilary Wainwright. Her enthusiasm and analyses have been inspirational.

My book strenuously attempts to avoid being a work of counterfactual history. I have never been remotely interested in a project of this type, although I can imagine that some readers might wish to interpret the work in this way. Instead, I am interested in contributing to ideas about the future of the labour and socialist movements in Britain, and perhaps even beyond our national boundaries. Hopefully, forthcoming projects will concentrate more on the future and less on the past than this book. For anyone interested, my article on a new socialist party in *Capital and Class* No 59 of Summer 1996 sets out some of my basic ideas on these subjects.

The choice of Sheffield for a case study of labourism is perhaps an obvious one. My personal and emotional links with the city, particularly its working-class and labourist culture, are very strong indeed. I think that this needs no further explanation here.

In the Sheffield chapter I have declined to refer to any theories regarding industrial change such as post-industrialism, post-fordism, flexible specialization, lean production, etc. simply because they are not relevant to this project. Instead, I am concerned with attempting to say something general about labourism and use the case study to try to illustrate this. In a sense then, it is not significant that I am looking specifically at the labour movement's responses to industrial decline and post-industrial developments. While, obviously, these things are of tremendous importance in themselves, my use of them is as an illustration of the ways that labourism operates generally. Therefore it is unnecessary to attempt to theorize and characterize the industrial changes that have taken place in Sheffield, and elsewhere, between the early 1970s and the present day.

The overall aim of the book is to attempt to characterize the ideas and actions of the labour movement from 1900 to the present day, and I use the term 'labourism' to denote this characterization. The choice of 1900 is obviously not accidental: it was the year that the Labour Representation Committee, which later became the Labour Party, was created. So, labourism is treated as continuous for the last 101 years and much of the book is aimed at justifying and substantiating this treatment. Of even more importance, though, is the contention that labourism has been ineffective on its own terms. This argument receives a great deal of attention and particular regard is paid to the issue of the party's aim being to gain electoral representation and the relative lack of success that it has had in its attempts to do this throughout the century. Thus, labourism is said to be continuous for the whole of the party's history and to account for its ineffectiveness.

The view of labourism presented here has seven principal characteristics: the absence of a clear, stated ideology; a confused and confusing policy-making process; 'pragmatism' over principles; attempting to appear national while in fact being sectional; a disingenuous emotional appeal; a lack of democracy and excessive bureaucracy and, finally, a culture of defeatism. These characteristics provide a structure for the whole book. They are introduced in the first chapter, appear throughout the second and third, and are given a detailed and comprehensive treatment in the conclusion.

As regards influences, the book draws most heavily upon Miliband's *Parliamentary Socialism: A Study in the Politics of Labour* (1972) but also on David Coates' two books (1975,1980), which look in detail at the policies and actions of the Labour governments of the 1960s and 1970s. In relatively recent times, Panitch and Leys' *The End of Parliamentary Socialism: From New Left to New Labour* (1997), which is itself an attempt to 'conclude' Miliband's book, was influential. All of these works are within a Marxist paradigm. My work, however, while heavily influenced by them, stands outside this tradition and, if a label has to be applied, belongs to an 'independent left' rather than to a specifically Marxist approach.

The first chapter examines the various characterizations and definitions of labourism on offer from a variety of authors, before providing an outline of my own view. The second chapter is a very selective history of the Labour Party which illustrates something of the general nature of labourism. The third chapter is an intensive empirical case study of the Sheffield labour movement from 1973 to 1998. It differs significantly from the other chapters in its methodology, which is empirical rather than text-based. Sixteen key members of the Sheffield labour movement were interviewed in an attempt to ascertain the nature of the movement's responses to the decline of steel and engineering and the rise of the service sector in the city. Finally, the conclusion aims to substantiate the characterization of labourism provided throughout the book.

Chapter 1
What is Labourism?

The Oxford English Dictionary defines labourism as the principles or tenets of the British Labour Party, and the holding or advocacy of them, without making any attempt to describe what these principles or tenets might be. This is tantamount to standing the quote, attributed to Lord Morrison of Lambeth: 'Socialism…is what a Labour government does'[1] on its head to become 'Labourism is what the Labour Party does'. While the former is simply not true, the latter is a truism. Nor is the term 'labourism' in common use, unlike, for example, the terms 'conservatism', 'liberalism' and even 'trade-unionism'. Why is it that labourism is hardly ever referred to in the media? The Labour Party has existed for over one hundred years, and the wider labour movement for considerably longer, so why is there no widespread use and understanding of the concept of labourism? In contrast, conservatism and liberalism, as ideas and phenomena, have a relatively widespread understanding and use.

Could any comparison be made with the fact that Margaret Thatcher achieved 'ism' status, as Prime Minister, while John Major did not? That is, that the principles that Mrs Thatcher stood for were clear and unmistakable, while Major clouded and obscured much of this clarity when he took over as Prime Minister. Tony Blair seems to have re-instated at least some of this clarity and would be well on his way to 'ism' status if it wasn't for the constant and widespread use of the term 'New Labour'. Or is it that we, as a population or electorate, have something of a general conception of the ideologies of conservatism, liberalism and socialism but do not equate labourism clearly with the latter? There is then a confusion about what labourism actually is, or what the concept means.

This chapter will begin by examining the thoughts of a large number of writers on the subject of labourism, before going on to the overall purpose of this book, which is to provide a possibly novel characterization of the concept. To begin with, only a possible outline or framework will be offered. This chapter, therefore, is an introduction to the subject of the book: what is the nature of labourism; why is there such a widespread ignorance of what it is; and can labourism account for and explain the ineffectiveness of the Labour Party? The latter point – the ineffectiveness of the party – is obviously highly contestable and will begin to be addressed in the account of the characteristics of labourism that appear at the end of this chapter. As already stated, these will offer only a preliminary outline at this stage, as the very question 'what is labourism?' is at the centre of the whole book. It is important to point out, however, that labourism is not being judged and evaluated against a hypothetical construct or alternative. Neither is the work one of counter-factual history, suggesting that if only the Labour Party had done something different, things would have turned out otherwise. Instead, the book looks at the question of the effectiveness of the party in terms of, and in relation to, its own aims and objectives. Thus, it will be evaluated as regards what it set out to do in 1900 and what it has subsequently, many times and in various ways, stated as its raison d'être. The question of the party's and movement's effectiveness will be examined in some detail in the concluding chapter of the book.

Many of the thoughts on labourism of the writers looked at in this chapter have common aspects. It is the differences between them, and the additional elements that they explore, that will be concentrated upon here.

Geoffrey Foote and Thomas Hodgskin[2]

According to Geoffrey Foote (1997), it was Thomas Hodgskin, in a pamphlet entitled *Labour Defended Against the Claims of Capital* (1825), who first elaborated a concept of labourism. This was a theory of trade union politics that employed Ricardo's labour theory of value to defend the emerging labour movement. Hodgskin thought that labourers were being cheated out of their rightful share of the surplus produce and that therefore the creation of trade unions was necessary to fight for this. While in favour of redistribution of wealth, he was, importantly, not opposed to capitalism as an economic and social system. Also, he believed that organised labour, independently of parliament, could achieve this redistribution and, again importantly, he perceived this in the context of the nation, sometimes protesting that imported Irish labourers, for example, brought down the wages of 'our' labourers.

For Foote, this 'trade union politics' represents the basis of labourism which informed the creation of the Labour Party. Parliament was merely substituted for independent trade union action. Like many commentators, Foote draws attention to the vague character of the party's ideology and also suggests that the Labour Party is a peculiarly British phenomenon: '...stressing specific policies to meet specific problems and only occasionally feeling the need to take its theorists seriously.'[3] He states that this conception of labourism was vague enough to unite liberals, trade unionists, Christian radicals and militant socialists in one party.

The relationship between the party and its trade union base offers the key to understanding labourism, suggests Foote. The social and political relationships between the Labour Party and the trade unions are the 'cornerstone' of labourism. Labourism is seen, purely and simply, as the politics of trade unionism. He believes that the characteristics of trade unions, which he takes from Hodgskin – their belief that labour receives little of the wealth it creates, their commitment to redistributionism, their hostility to capitalists (but not capitalism), their commitment to workers self-reliance and their loyalty to nation-state – have all survived and become a set of assumptions within the labour movement. They '...constitute the fundamental labourist tenets of the Labour Party'.[4]

These very early characteristics of labourism provided by Hodgskin are quite different to the seven cited at the end of this chapter. However, they do represent something of a foundation for what follows. The facts that 175 years have elapsed since the publication of Hodgskin's pamphlet and that the Labour Party has existed for the last 101 of them are also obviously of great significance.

For Foote, as for Hodgskin, labourism has its limits. It is distinct from revolutionary and anti-nationalist ideologies on its left and from liberalism on its right. However, within these limits it is flexible and ideologically wide-ranging. Many commentators would, at least partly, agree with Foote that the politics of the trade-unionism of the nineteenth century form the basis of labourism, but would, crucially, add a number of further, very important elements to the concept. This can be seen as we go on to look at the thoughts on the subject of others, particularly Miliband (1972), Saville (1973, 1988), Coates (1975, 1980, 1989), Nairn (1964) and Thompson (1993). But first we will turn to the views on labourism of Theodore Rothstein (1929).

Theodore Rothstein[5]

Moving on more than one hundred years after Hodgskin, we will very briefly examine the comments of Rothstein in his book *From Chartism to Labourism: Historical Sketches of the English Working Class Movement* (1929). Beginning with Chartism, which he describes as the start of 'The political class movement of the modern proletariat…'[6], Rothstein traces the path of this movement to the creation of the Labour Representation Committee (LRC) in 1900. As regards the latter, he is clearly not very impressed: '…in selecting the name for the new movement, or rather for the permanent joint committee of trade union- ists and Socialists to be appointed by the conference, it was decided to adopt the modest name of Labour Representation Committee, without emphasising the independent character of the Representation, and only five years later the name of Labour Party was adopted, again without further adjectives. All of this was quite in keeping with the policy of following the line of least resistance.'[7] It is lack of independence from the Liberals that Rothstein is drawing our attention to here. He suggests that co-operation with the Liberals was implicit within the creation of the LRC. We will return to this point in our examination of Miliband below and in the next chapter.

This co-operation, which he refers to as '…the humble role of the wagging tail of the Liberal Party.'[8], is central to Rothstein's characteriza- tion of labourism. In fact, apart from in the title of his book, he does not use the term 'labourism', preferring instead 'opportunism'! However, in the final chapter of his book, which examines the first fifteen years of the twentieth century, he makes it quite clear what he thinks of the Labour Party: 'The working class…made peace with bourgeois society, although struggling from time to time against its more flagrant abuses…This was the period of stagnation in the English Labour movement and of the complete captivity of the minds of the workers by vulgar bourgeois ideology…'[9]

Rothstein's left-wing, revolutionary politics clearly have a bearing as regards his dismissive attitude to the Labour Party. The writers we will now go on to examine are, generally, much more engaged with debates about the nature of the party.

WHAT IS LABOURISM?

Ralph Miliband[10]

In relatively recent times, Ralph Miliband is the first person to have used and developed a concept of labourism. In *Parliamentary Socialism, A Study in the Politics of Labour* (1972), he introduces it in his comments on the inclusion of Clause Four in the Labour Party's new constitution: 'In 1918, the Labour Party's commitment to socialism on the basis of common ownership, which the Labour Left had so long desired, seemed unambiguous enough to raise lively hopes that Labour had finally done with its own version of Liberalism. And so in fact it had. But what had replaced it was not socialism, but Labourism, of which the Labour Party's statement of policy, *Labour and the New Social Order* of 1918, was the manifesto.'[11] Miliband's main criticism of this document is that it reaffirmed the party's commitment to capitalism, with intervention by the state being seen as a guarantee of social justice. Instead of attempting to replace capitalism with socialism, Labour was aiming at a more advanced and more regulated form of capitalism. However, he does concede that the proposals contained within it, on public ownership, health, education, full employment and social services, all to be financed by progressive taxation, were a huge step forward for the party and, according to him, it was this promise that persuaded the socialists within the party to accept it. For Miliband, the 1918 constitution and the party's new statement of policy represented its first comprehensive appearance as the advocate of state intervention to regulate private enterprise so as to humanize and stabilize capitalism and provide employment and welfare for working men and women. It is this, although Miliband does not explicitly state it here, that he conceives of as the ideological basis of labourism.

Miliband can be criticized for not providing a definition of labourism and instead appearing to adopt a negative conception of it: merely that labourism is 'not socialism'. Miliband does not, in Parliamentary Socialism or anywhere else, provide us with a definition of labourism. However, despite this, a careful reading of his book renders an elaboration of the concept that is comprehensive, consistent and, in fact, not merely a negative one.

It has also been said by, amongst others, Tom Forester (1976), John Marriott (1991) and Willie Thompson (1993), that Miliband concentrates almost exclusively on Labour's commitment to parliamentary means of political activity over any other forms, and it is true that he does emphasize this very important aspect of labourism. On the very first page of the introduction to *Parliamentary Socialism*, he writes: '...the leaders of the Labour Party have always rejected any kind of political action (such as industrial action for political purposes) which fell, or appeared to them to fall, outside the framework and convention of the parliamentary system. The Labour Party has not only been a parliamentary party; it has been a party deeply imbued by parliamentarianism.'[12] However, his conception of labourism is not restricted merely to the party's concentration on parliament over any other forms of political action. The development of his argument throughout the book, concentrating on the empirical rather than the abstract as it does, is much more complex. His is essentially a critical examination of the history and development of the party from 1900 until the time of his writing, with a postscript added in 1972 detailing further developments in the 1960s. He examines, in some detail, the major events of that whole period, plus some of the lesser ones, and out of this emerges a characterization of the party.

It must be emphasized that Miliband stresses the continuity of the nature of the Labour Party right throughout its history. For him, the party was essentially the same in 1972 as it was in 1918. This characterization has a number of key points. The most important of these is what might be termed Labour's 'vagueness of purpose'. The events that led to the formation of the Labour Representation Committee (LRC) in 1900 have been relatively well documented by Pelling (1965, 1982), amongst others. The Independent Labour Party (ILP), which had been founded seven years earlier, was instrumental in the creation of the LRC. One of its leading members, Keir Hardie, was very keen to see representation of working people in parliament, independent of the existing political parties. Thus he, and a number of other leading members of the ILP, including Ramsay MacDonald, persuaded a number of trade union leaders to press the Trades Union Congress (TUC) to support a conference to discuss the formation of what later became the LRC. At its founding conference in 1900 the committee adopted the following statement as its purpose: '...a distinct Labour group in Parliament, who shall have their own whips, and agree upon their policy, which must embrace a readiness to cooperate with any party which for the time being may be engaged in promoting legislation in the direct interests of labour, and be equally ready to associate themselves with any party in opposing measures having an opposite tendency.'[13]

The Fabian Society and the Social Democratic Federation (SDF) both played much more peripheral roles in the creation of the LRC: the first because it did not at this stage support independent labour representation, preferring 'permeation' of the Liberal Party instead, and the second because it was extremely disappointed with the new organization's refusal to even acknowledge the existence of the class war. The SDF withdrew from the LRC in disgust one year after its formation.

According to Miliband, the ILP's compromise with the trade unions in not insisting upon socialism as the aim of the new organization, represents the first and fateful act that would lead to the later creation of 'labourism'. He writes: 'In order to make possible an alliance with the trade unions, the Socialists of the ILP were content to agree that the new body should only declare its purpose to be the representation of working-class opinion 'by men sympathetic with the aims and demands of the Labour movement', and to leave those aims and demands undefined.'[14] His view of this compromise is absolutely crucial to his conception of the Labour Party and the labour movement. The idea of an organization whose aims are representation without any specification of the nature of that representation is absolutely central to Miliband's characterization. This vagueness of purpose continues right throughout the party's history. It is also absolutely central to the characterization of labourism being advanced in this book and will be returned to in the second chapter.

At least part of the reason for the aims of the LRC being left undefined was that most of the trade unionists attending the founding conference were radical liberal rather than socialist in political orientation, and Miliband stresses this influence throughout. After only a few months of existence the LRC was seeking electoral agreements with the Liberal Party. As already seen, he suggests that this liberalism, admittedly of the radical variety, was eventually replaced by labourism in 1918.

The decision to pursue parliamentary means of political action over other forms was based on the perception, by trade union and other labour leaders, of the persistent failure of industrial action. A court case, *Lyons v. Wilkins*, had, in the 1890s, seriously restricted the right of trade unions to picket during a strike. This, plus a number of other cases, persuaded these trade union and labour leaders to pursue the course of independent labour representation in parliament. Some thought that the court's and the House of Lords' decisions against them on these legal matters were political in nature. This perception added weight to the argument for labour representation in parliament. The main supporters of this view were the leaders of the new unskilled unions whose very existence were threatened by this legislation. They felt that parliamentary representation could make their future existence more secure.

However, it is not the decision to pursue independent parliamentary representation in itself that Miliband criticizes. It is the sole concentration on parliament over any other forms of political action that he objects to. He demonstrates that the Labour Party has consistently chosen exclusively parliamentary activity over any other forms, right throughout its history. The General Strike of 1926 was the most blatant example of this, with Labour's industrial and political leaders calling off the strike without any conditions or guarantees from the employers or government. Miliband's comments on this illustrate a very important aspect of his whole conception of labourism: 'The Labour movement was betrayed, but not because the Labour leaders were villains, or cowards. It was betrayed because betrayal was the inherent and inescapable consequence of their whole philosophy of politics – and it would be quite foolish to think that their philosophy was the less firmly held for being unsystematically articulated.'[15] So, for him, this capacity for 'betrayal' of the movement by its leaders represents an integral characteristic of labourism. It can be seen, throughout its history, that the party and movement has re-enacted this scenario, in different ways at different times, over and over again. MacDonald's 'great betrayal' of 1931 was only the extreme and logical consequence of this. This will be termed, within this book, the 'logic of labourism'.

The apparent contradiction here – that the logic of labourism dictates that its leaders will always 'betray' the movement – is reflected by, and linked to, another contradiction. According to Miliband, the party's link with the trade unions means that it is a 'class party', yet its leaders have consistently and comprehensively insisted upon and promoted the idea that the party is a 'national' one, appealing to all sections of society. This is as true of Tony Blair as it was of Ramsay MacDonald. In January 1924, at a rally at the Albert Hall in London celebrating the beginning of the first ever Labour government, MacDonald said that he was not '...thinking of party; I am thinking of national well-being...'.[16] Miliband insists that this was not seen to be compatible with the pursuit of working-class 'well-being'. In September 1996, speaking to the TUC

General Council on the relationship between the trade unions and the Labour Party, Blair said: 'You make a case for your members, to which we listen in opposition and to which we will listen in government. But our job is to govern for the whole nation',[17] and at the party's Welsh conference in February 1997 he referred to Labour as a '...one nation party...'[18]

The Labour Party did emerge '...out of the bowels of the trade unions'[19] as Ernest Bevin so succinctly put it, and has continued its life as a party that is inextricably linked with the unions. This relationship, as Lewis Minkin (1991) and others have correctly observed, has not been an easy-going one and, in fact, has been fraught with tensions and difficulties. At present the link is apparently under direct threat from a Blair leadership committed to significantly weakening it, if not breaking it altogether. Not withstanding these things, the party's links with the unions makes the leadership's claims to be a party of and in the national interest appear at best vacuous and at worst false. So, here is the second contradiction we have examined regarding the nature of the Labour Party: it has emerged from the trade unions and has consistently preserved its link with them throughout its history, yet its leaders have always claimed that it is a 'national' party. Miliband further infers that this link with the trade unions means that it is therefore a 'class party', thus equating trade union interests with class interests. While this book has little to say on the subject, it does not equate trade union and class. However, importantly, it does recognize the important conflict between sectional and national interests.

In summary, the main points of Miliband's conception of labourism are: the compromise between the ILP and the trade unions in 1900 based upon the vagueness of purpose of the new organization and the persistence of this throughout the party's history; the political influence of radical liberalism; the concentration upon parliamentary activity to the exclusion of any other forms of political action; the inherent logic of betrayal of the movement by its leaders, and the contradiction of Labour presenting itself as a 'national' party while in reality being a 'class' party.

It would be reasonable to criticize Miliband because he concentrates upon the thoughts and activities of the leaders of the labour movement and virtually ignores the ideas, events and action at the level of the ordinary membership. In fact, he acknowledges this himself in the introduction to his book. However, it should be stressed that his very conception of the movement and party includes the notion of the enormous power and influence that their leaders possess. Thus, the criticisms that he makes are valid: the power of its leaders mean that, in most instances, they are, or at least are perceived to be, the party and movement. The characterization presented in this book will agree with this idea, regrettable though it is.

Miliband's book has been examined at such length because his is easily the most important conception of labourism, and is the one upon which many of the subsequent thinkers base their deliberations. Again, it should be noted that for him the Labour Party is characterized by continuity and has been faced by very similar problems right throughout its history. He writes: 'Like Hobbes and fear, crisis and the Labour Party have always been twins – Siamese twins.'[20] Hence 'labourism' characterizes the party, throughout its history since 1918.

John Saville[21]

Unlike Miliband, John Saville does provide us with an actual definition of labourism: 'Labourism, as it developed through the third quarter of the nineteenth century, was a theory and practice which accepted the possibility of social change within the existing framework of society; which rejected the revolutionary violence and action implicit in Chartist ideas of physical force; and which increasingly recognised the working of political democracy of the parliamentary variety as the practical means of achieving its own aims and objectives. Labourism was the theory and practice of class collaboration; it was a tradition which in theory (always) and in practice (mostly) emphasized the unity of Capital and Labour, and the importance of conciliation and arbitration in industrial disputes.'[22] He suggests that the ethos of labourism is summed up in the expression 'a fair day's pay for a fair day's work'.

Saville, like Rothstein, traces the 'roots' of labourism to the demise of Chartism and the concomitant domination of working men by bourgeois ideology. Thus labourism stepped in to provide a 'medium' or a 'bridge' for the transmission of this ideology. Like Miliband, he also notes contradictions within labourism: between the bitter struggles of workers in factories, workshops and mines in the latter half of the nineteenth century and the public pronouncements of their leaders which often stressed the need for partnerships between Labour and Capital. Incidentally, this notion of 'partnership' informs the approach of the

New Labour government in the late 1990s and early twenty-first century, perhaps suggesting continuity with the past rather than the radical break it claims to represent – much more of which later in the book.

Illustrating his arguments with the paradox of the miners' strong class solidarity and yet unswerving loyalty to parliamentary representation, Saville presents a powerful conception of labourism as deeply rooted in the traditions of British industrial society and its working class. For him, this explains the failure of socialist ideas to take hold in Britain. After the collapse of Chartism such ideas disappeared completely until their return in the 1880s. By that time labourism had such a strong hold over the working class that socialism was either incorporated into it, thereby losing its force, or completely rejected.

He repeats many of these ideas in *The Labour Movement in Britain* (1988). Additionally, he makes the point that labourism was more prevalent amongst the skilled working population, was male-dominated, and, as regards social issues, was deeply conservative. The radicalism of the Owenites on gender, the family and religion had disappeared by the 1870s. He also writes: 'The ideology of labourism encouraged working people to maintain their sense of class, another way of describing their independence and self-respect; but it also involved the acceptance of a subordinate role in political society.'[23] Saville links this subordination back to the successful transmission of 'the dominant ideology'.

David Coates[24]
David Coates quotes Saville's definition of labourism in *The Labour Party and the Struggle for Socialism* (1975) and suggests that this is what Keir Hardie meant when he referred to labourism at the founding conference of the LRC. In a later work, *Labour in Power? A Study of the Labour Government 1974-1979* (1980), Coates, who was very influenced by Miliband, draws attention to the labourist denial of the incompatibility of labour and capital and its equation of politics with parliamentary activity. These things have made trade union leaders vulnerable to calls for moderation, 'in the national interest', from both Labour and Conservative governments. Coates claims that this is as true of the late 1970s as it was during the General Strike of 1926. Continuing with a number of the points made by Miliband, he writes: 'The dominant political perspective amongst large sections of the British labour

movement has been, and remains, 'Labourist'. By that I mean first that workers have taken the wage relationship under capitalism as unalterable, and have concentrated upon improving their lot within it. In addition, the belief has predominated that politics is about parliamentary action; and any widespread knowledge of, or interest in, extra-parliamentary forms of working-class political activity has been limited. Moreover, although the language of the British labour movement has been the language of 'class', there has rarely been any generalised sense of class as an antagonistic, as distinct from defensive, community...'[25]

In *The Crisis of Labour* (1989), Coates offers us an even more comprehensive definition: 'LABOURISM is a term which...is meant to capture the dominant definitions of 'the political' enshrined in the political philosophy and practice of the Labour Party since 1900, and of its predecessor working class political organisations (mainly on the left wing of the Gladstonian Liberal Party). A 'Labourist' reading of working class political interests emphasises their discrete and limited nature, their attainability within capitalism, and their capacity for realisation through parliamentary channels. Labourism is to be contrasted, and saw itself as distinct from, and in competition with, both less radical and more revolutionary specifications of working class political interests: standing in opposition both to Conservative denials of any distinctly 'working class' political interests which required a separate working class party, and in opposition to revolutionary socialist arguments that working class political interests could only be realised by the total replacement of capitalism and its dominant classes.'[26] So, according to this quote, Labour represented a 'third way' over one hundred years ago!

Coates has been cited at length for two reasons. First, because he provides us, in the quoted text, with very comprehensive definitions of labourism. Second, because a number of the points that he makes are of specific interest. For example, unlike Miliband, who dates the inception of labourism from 1918, Coates takes it back, even before the foundation of the LRC, to the radical wing of the late-nineteenth-century Liberal Party. But the most important overall point, present in both Coates' and Saville's work, is the idea that labourism developed, as an ideology and political practice, in opposition to other forms of ideology and political practice. Perhaps this goes some way to explaining the somewhat negative approach of labour leaders, past and present. They are against conservatism, elements of liberalism and revolutionary socialism but what are they actually *for*? Historically this has been an issue for writers on the Labour Party and labour movement, and continues to be so right up to the present day. What does the current Labour government actually stand for and, going beyond policy considerations, what are the principles that are guiding its decisions and policy formulation? The difficulties that one has in answering these questions perhaps goes some way to explaining why the term 'labourism' is not in common use: if not based on positive principles, a political practice has little meaning. This was true of the Labour Party, and indeed the wider labour movement, for the whole of the last century, if not longer. Miliband drew our attention to this as regards the inception of the party in 1900. This book will argue that this vagueness of purpose has persisted since then and is an essential characteristic of labourism.

Tom Nairn[27]

In two articles appearing in the *New Left Review* in 1964, entitled *The Nature of the Labour Party*, Tom Nairn approaches the subject from a slightly different perspective. He emphasises three key factors in the early development of the Labour Party: the influence of Victorian trade-unionism; the influence of Fabianism and the party's 'anti-intellectualism'. The Labour Party perceived itself to be the logical development of trade union thought and action. Crucially, Nairn argues that this is false because, by its very nature, a political party should be involved in hegemonic issues which relate to a whole society.

His is a damning critique of the creation and development of the Labour Party. On the 'indigenous theories' of socialism, particularly Fabianism, he writes: 'They adapted and transformed third-rate bourgeois traditions into fourth-rate socialist traditions, imposing upon the working class all the righteous mediocrity and worthless philistinism of the pious Victorian petty bourgeois.'[28] This also applies to the socialism of the ILP which he dramatically refers to as: '...the cadaver passed on to the Labour movement.'[29]

Where Nairn differs significantly from the previous writers is in his concentration on the anti-intellectualism and scarcity of ideas in the labour movement. He writes: 'If the ideas of Fabianism were few and tedious, this post-Christian socialism (referring to the ILP) had no ideas at all.'[30] He shares with Foote and others the view that labourism was an evolutionary development from trade union politics: the Labour Party was merely a trade union pressure group. Nairn examines the dynamic of labourism in detail and suggests that it alienates the socialist activist and reassures Conservatives.

He sums up: 'Labourism was the product, the incarnation, of class stasis and intellectual stasis; it was the negation of any moving dynamic between theory and practice, the heavy domination of practice – in certain precise historically established forms – over theory and consciousness.'[31] This anti-theory and general anti-intellectualism was also touched upon by Foote and is one of the main subjects of a book by Radikha Desai, *Intellectuals and Socialism* (1994), which we will examine very briefly later.

Tom Forester[32]

Like Miliband Tom Forester (1976) draws attention to the 'vagueness of purpose' at the formation of the LRC. The motion that was put to the TUC Conference in 1899, calling for a special conference, stated its aim as ...securing a better representation of the interests of labour in the House of Commons.[33] Forester suggests that the decision, to leave the aims of the new organization unstated contributed towards the later 'freedom' of the Parliamentary Labour Party, the party's lack of concern with ideologies and programmes, an implicit belief in the aims of the labour movement and the placing of the party within the traditions of the British constitution and political culture. It is suggested that this broad, undogmatic approach was more in keeping with the British political character than a doctrinaire approach. He acknowledges that there is no agreed definition of labourism and that it is often used as a term of abuse. He draws our attention to Lichtheim's use of the term to describe the working class's instinctive sense of separateness, rather than its desire to remodel society in its own image.

Forester makes a series of distinctions between labourism and socialism as world-views, suggesting that the former is passive while the latter is active, reflexive compared to educative, empirical rather than ideological, pragmatic rather than principled, evolutionary as opposed to revolutionary, practical rather than intellectual and has an 'ethic of responsibility' while socialism has an 'ethic of ultimate ends'. But he is keen to point out that these do not imply criticism or even value judgement. Instead, they support the idea of the Labour Party as realistic in its aims within the context of the traditions of British political culture. He

emphasizes the distinctive 'Britishness' of labourism, with its shared attitudes with other political parties and bourgeois society, and singles out the
Fabians as the intellectuals of the labour movement. Their role in
promoting empiricism and evolution was crucial. He concludes that the
Labour Party was more the product and instrument of history than its
creator. Very importantly though, he does not intend this is as a criticism
but views it simply a reflection of British political culture. In this respect,
he distances himself from writers such as Miliband, Coates and Nairn.

We will now look at a number of writers who have somewhat
different or unusual perspectives on the concept of labourism.

Stephen Haseler[34]

Stephen Haseler (1980) has a novel approach to the subject. His is an
unashamed support for labourism, which he sees as '...merely an aspect
of the more general British liberal tradition dressed up to express the
emergence of a new interest in the land, a new sociological outgrowth of
industrial Britain.'[35] In contrast, socialism, as an ideology and a political
practice, has had virtually no influence on the British working class and
its 'authentic' leaders. *Labour's success has occurred precisely because it has
distanced itself from socialism.* Haseler contrasts this labourism, which he
sees as desirable and totally in keeping with British political traditions
and the aspirations of the working class and which characterized the
Labour Party up until the first half of the 1970s, with what it then
became – a party dominated by the left and with a labourist tradition
degenerated into careerism. Thus the centre-right had become bureaucratic and the left – dangerous and vulgar – had taken over the party.

Haseler differs from the other writers examined here in that he cele-
brates labourism as a proud British tradition which has been destroyed
by the 'bureaucratization' of the labour movement and the space that this
created for the ascent of the Labour Left in the 1970s. He predicts the
election of a socialist government at the end of the 1980s which, he
believes, would be a tragedy for Britain.

John Marriott

John Marriott also approaches the subject from a novel and inter-
esting perspective in his book *The Culture of Labourism, The East End
Between the Wars* (1990). In fact, the sub-title is slightly misleading as
Marriott concentrates exclusively on West Ham. He begins by looking

at definitions of labourism, interestingly suggesting that none on offer are satisfactory and therefore that he hopes to arrive at his own definition or, at least, to establish the 'boundaries' of labourism.

Since Miliband's *Parliamentary Socialism*, writes Marriott, there has been a tendency to equate labourism with parliamentary activity, and therefore with the party rather than the movement. Writers such as Nairn (1964), Forester (1976), Haseler (1980) and Panitch (1986) have all emphasized parliamentarianism and the distance between the Labour Party and socialism. They have concentrated on the party at the national level. Marriott suggests that these studies implied that what was happening at the local level was merely a reflection of the national level. He takes issue with this and claims that 'Working-class politics is located in a wider material, cultural and social universe, and has no meaning outside that universe. Moreover, for the vast majority of the working class, certainly for the period with which this study is concerned, the universe was strongly bounded by local factors.'[36] So, Marriott concentrates on the local where previous studies of labourism concentrated on the national. He examines the working-class culture of labourism which, he suggests, has been underestimated in importance: 'Labourism is not to be understood merely in its institutions and strategies; it emerged from and is rooted within lived social and material relationships.'[37]

His is a detailed empirical study of the labour movement in West Ham and is a very welcome addition to the literature on labourism. In conclusion, Marriott attempts to provide an answer to the question '...did the party succeed in becoming a vital component of popular culture within West Ham?'[38] While Labour completely dominated formal politics in West Ham (after the moves against communist influence in the first half of the 1920s), did this support permeate the culture of working-class West Ham? 'No', answers Marriott: electoral support was low and membership of the party was pitiful. In 1929, West Ham Labour Party, where electoral success was unparalleled, had only 720 members compared with Greenwich with 1500 and Woolwich with 4971 where Labour's electoral success was not as impressive. *Political activity amongst the electorate was lowest in the safest Labour seats.*

Marriott locates the explanation for this in the social and political culture of the dominant group – unskilled manual workers. He arrives at the conclusion that those people with no involvement in the institutions of the labour movement, the unskilled working-class, supported the Labour Party in a vague, instinctive way and other parties, when they have made a concerted effort, have made inroads into the Labour Party's dominance. This then, for Marriott, constitutes the 'limits of labourism'.

Willie Thompson[39]

Willie Thompson, in his enigmatically titled book *The Long Death of British Labourism* (1993), again takes a slightly different look at the subject. Starting with a neutral definition of labourism as '...the organising principles, ethos, perceptions and socio-political project of...the British labour movement',[40] he goes on to note that 'Labourism is therefore an orientation towards a certain social and political reality and not necessarily articulated in any coherent or theoretical fashion.'[41] He also argues, importantly, that even those tendencies within the labour movement that are explicitly antagonistic to labourism have been absorbed within it.

Like many of the commentators looked at here, he traces the roots of labourism to the trade unionism of skilled manual workers of the 1850s and '60s. However, moving on to discuss the formation of the Labour Party, he takes issue with Miliband's concentration on government office, arguing that in itself this should not constitute a problem and that it can go hand-in-hand with other forms of mobilisation and support. Thompson is absolutely correct here: there is no *a priori* reason why involvement in parliamentary and local government activity should constitute a weakness or a problem for a social democratic or socialist party and Miliband is not suggesting that this is the case. It is the exclusivity of parliamentary means of political action that he objects to. However, Thompson agrees with Miliband that this involvement, in reality, has constituted a fundamental problem and weakness as regards the British Labour Party.

Thompson concentrates on the reverence that the labour movement has for the institutions of the state. This was, ultimately, its undoing. He identifies an authoritarianism as a central characteristic of labourism, whose form, he suggests, it shares with the right wing. Thus it was unable to resist the onslaught from Thatcherism on the welfare state, the trade unions and local government. Along with Elliott (1993), Thompson, who was also writing in 1993, suggests that labourism is already dead, killed by this relentless attack from the right, which severed its links with the state. Thompson's diagnosis does seem premature in the light of the electoral success of Blair's 'New Labour' in 1997.

Gregory Elliott[42]

Despite his book's title, Gregory Elliott, in *Labourism and the English Genius. The Strange Death of Labour England?* (1993), does not elaborate a concept of labourism. Nevertheless, he makes some fascinating observations on the nature of the Labour Party; for example – 'Neither meaningfully socialist, nor coherently social-democratic, Labour has been only fitfully – and then feebly – *democratic*, or politically reformist. Accommodated within an old constitutional settlement that had been forged for pre-democratic purposes, and whose genius lay in the neutralization by absorption of democratic impulses, Labour was seduced into its own betrayal.'[43] This statement encapsulates his central argument: that acceptance of the *ancien regime* has proved to be fatal to labourism. While being as critical as most of the writers examined in this chapter, Elliott approaches the subject from a different perspective: that of the death of an idea of 'England' based on a traditional nationalist and imperialist approach. Thus he congratulates the British ruling class for helping to shape a loyal opposition in its own image; one which, when intermittently presented with the opportunity to govern, can be completely trusted with the institutions and traditions of the British state. He concludes by noting the passing of this notion of 'England'.

Radhika Desai[44]

In an important book, *Intellectuals and Socialism, 'Social Democrats' and the Labour Party* (1994), Radhika Desai builds upon Nairn's criticism of Labour as '...a profoundly unintellectual party...'.[45] For her, though, the main intellectual current in the party was revisionism and its main opponent within the Labour Party was, and still is, unintellectual labourism. She suggests that the term denotes '...Labour's imperviousness to philosophies or ideas in general.'[46] Citing Nairn, for whom it had this specific meaning which differed from other views on the left, she adopts this approach. In place of intellectualism, the party placed pragmatism and the power of the conference. Initially this favoured revisionism, benefiting from the alliance between Attlee and the trade union leaders which controlled the party conference from 1949 onwards. This alliance proved important when the revisionist Gaitskell took over as party leader in 1955. Gaitskell strengthened the link with the unions by acting strongly against communism in the labour movement. However, this alliance proved fragile and came apart over his attempts to get rid of Clause Four and his failure to win the party conference back to his anti-unilateralist stance on nuclear disarmament.

So, for Desai labourism represents an unintellectualism that permeates the party, left, right and centre and is impervious to ideas of any kind. Her definition differs substantially from the others discussed here. Even Nairn does not concentrate exclusively on the party's intellectual status.

Michael Barratt-Brown and Colin Leys[47]

Michael Barratt-Brown (1972) and Colin Leys (1989) use the term 'labourism' differently. Barratt-Brown uses it in the title of his book *From Labourism to Socialism: The Political Economy in the 1970s* and then does not use it again anywhere in the book. Regarding his concept of labourism, it can only be assumed that he is referring to the ideology and political practice of the Labour Party and is contrasting it, by inference in the title, with socialism. In fact, Barratt-Brown is arguing for a movement away from the labourism of the past and encouraging the party and trade unions to embrace socialist theory and practice.

In contrast, Colin Leys traces the term back to the foundation of the Labour Representation Committee and the ILP's rejection of socialism as one of its objectives. He writes: '…the workers did not yet support the idea of socialism. The ILP believed that once the workers supported an independent party of labour, support for socialism would grow out of the struggle for reforms.'[48] Leys, turning Miliband 'on his head', argues that the introduction of Clause Four in the party's 1918 constitution was the result of the industrial conflict before the First World War and was a direct challenge to the labourism that had dominated the party's policy up till then. He concedes, though, that by 1918 labourism was well entrenched in the party and was supported by parliamentarianism and the lack of a formal extra-parliamentary base for the party. Thus the challenge to it was unsuccessful.

However, Leys sees the history of the Labour Party up until approximately 1981 as '…the history of the gradual radicalisation of the labour movement.'[49] He argues that slowly but surely it moved away from its liberal-labourist beginnings and, by the early 1980s, had arrived at a point where its demands were becoming incompatible with capitalism. Thus, he suggests that the events and activities within the labour movement in the early 1980s were the product of a prolonged move away from labourism towards socialism that had been taking place since 1918. Writing in 1989 he predicts optimistically that the party '...might yet become a socialist party.'[50]

Both Barratt-Brown and Leys have a similar view of labourism: essentially that it is not socialism and that the latter would be a much more desirable aim for the Labour Party.

Hilary Wainwright[51]

Hilary Wainwright is one of the most important thinkers and activists on the British independent left. In a number of publications, most notably *Labour: A Tale of Two Parties* (1987), *Arguments for a New Left* (1994) and in an article in *Socialist Register* ('Once More Moving On', 1995), she has consistently argued a position which, while to the left of the Labour Party, does not preclude the possibilities for progress that it presents. She writes: 'The political values of Labourism stem from the combination of the values of trade unionism with those of parliamentary respectability...The political values of Labourism, generalising from the imperatives of trade-union organisation, tend to hold up political unity as paramount, at the expense of initiative and innovation, and to place loyalty before independence and critical debate.'[52] Wainwright suggests that the left-wing developments within the party, through the late 1960s and 1970s, represent a break with this labourism, a view with which this book does not concur, more of which later.

She also provides a more extensive description: 'The British Labour Party never was in a full sense a social democratic party. As a creature of one of the strongest trade union movements in the world, it has had a dual and at times chimerical character.

On the one hand, as formally 'the party of the working class', it appears, especially at times of working-class militancy, to have the potential to bring about radical reforms – far more radical than the reforms of a continental social democratic party lacking direct links with workers' organization... On the other hand, the character of these linkages (in particular the fact that the locus's of power lie with the leadership of trade unions and parliamentary parties rather than, say, with the workplace organizations, local constituency parties and MPs) are shaped by the origins of the party as, literally, the Representation Committee of the trade unions.'[53]

Other writers

This chapter has examined writers who work with an active concept of labourism. Clearly, there are many others who have much to say about the nature of the Labour Party and wider labour movement, some of which coincides with aspects of the characterizations examined here. Leo Panitch, Stuart Hall, Eric Hobsbawm and David Howell come to mind as the most important. Their ideas have not been explored because we are looking specifically at concepts of labourism. However, it is worth referring very briefly to some of their ideas on the subject of the Labour Party and movement.

Panitch (1976) draws attention to the following: 'Ever since its founding conference threw out a motion calling for 'a distinct party...based on the recognition of the class war', the Party has presented itself as a *national* party cast in the historical role of integrating the interests and demands of the working class with those of the British nation as a whole.'[54] He makes much of this notion of Labour as an 'integrative' rather than a class party and makes a not dissimilar point ten years later: 'When a party like the British Labour Party finally committed itself to socialism in the sense of clause four – the taking into public ownership of the means of production, distribution and exchange – it never answered the question that arose over how this could be achieved while at the same time retaining its long-standing commitment to class cooperation as opposed to class struggle.'[55]

In 1997 Panitch and Colin Leys published an extremely comprehensive book detailing the shift from the 'new left' within the Labour Party of the late 1960s and 1970s to the appearance of 'New Labour' in the 1990s. Entitled *The End of Parliamentary Socialism*, it attempts to write the conclusion to Miliband's *Parliamentary Socialism* (1972). The book is engaged in presenting the Labour left throughout the 1970s and early 1980s as the true modernising force and Blair et al as 'neo-liberals'. It will not be examined further here because it does not provide a characterization of labourism but instead relies on Miliband's '..."dogmatic adherence" to a conventionally narrow brand of parliamentarianism.'[56]

Stuart Hall has been more interested in analysing the popularity of Thatcherism than looking at the Labour Party and movement, But he has occasionally turned his mind to examining the latter, for example in his essay 'The Crisis of Labourism' (Hall, 1988). This essay is mainly anecdotal and fails to provide a characterization of labourism. However, in an earlier article in the collection, 'The Great Moving Right Show', he does offer the following: '..."Labourism", or Labour socialism, has been marked from its origins by its Fabian-collectivist inheritance. The expansion of the state machine, under the management of state servants and experts, has often been defined in this tradition as synonymous with socialism itself. Labour has been willing to use this state to reform conditions for working people, provided this did not bite too deeply into the "logic" of capitalist accumulation. But it has refused like the plague the mobilization of democratic power at the popular level.'[57] Hall's thoughts will not be examined further here as he tends to have a somewhat superficial, and perhaps even naïve, view of labourism, as shown by his comments in another essay in the same collection: '...reformism is not only a long and important tradition. Actually, it has always been the dominant tradition within the Labour Party itself. But is not socialism.'[58] This idea of labourism as 'reformism' is a very simplistic notion that many on the British Left subscribe to. It involves a conflation of 'social democracy' with reformism. There is also the question of whether labourism is the British form of social democracy, which will be returned to later.

The historian Eric Hobsbawm has built his intellectual career on examining and analysing the labour movement and party. In recent times he is associated within the labour movement with the book *Forward March of Labour Halted?* (1981), which developed from his 1978 Marx Memorial Lecture of the same name. His central argument will not be examined here as it is not directly relevant. However, it is worth mentioning that the assumption underlying his thesis is that the Labour Party represents the political expression of 'the working-class', which he equates with trade unionism.[59] David Howell (1980) does not provide us with a characterization of labourism, which he refers to as 'British Social Democracy'. His overall approach is empirically-based, so perhaps this is not totally surprising.

Some brief criticisms

Most of the writers examined here offer powerful and convincing conceptions of labourism, largely based on that of Miliband. However, even taken together, they do not form a fully comprehensive characterization of labourism that would, for example, adequately explain its absence as a concept in common use. Much more importantly, they fail to provide a characterization that deals appropriately and adequately with the question of the effectiveness of the Labour Party and labour movement throughout the last 101 years.

After all, the question of effectiveness must arise in relation to a party whose overriding aim is to be a party of parliamentary representation and yet has managed to form a government for only twenty-five of the 101 years that it has been in existence, and then for only nineteen years as a majority government. Such a low success rate would be the subject of scrutiny in any other walk of life. Thus, the party is being evaluated in relation to its own stated aim of parliamentary representation of working people.

Miliband's characterization is the most comprehensive and many of his points are developed in this book. However, he overemphasizes the problem of Labour's adherence to parliamentary representation in favour of 'industrial action'. The fundamental problem is not the commitment to parliamentary representation but the absence of any description of its content. This same criticism can be extended to David Coates. For both writers, the 'class struggle' outside parliament, particularly in the form of 'industrial action', was seen as of paramount importance. This book will suggest that it was not a matter of favouring parliamentary activity over industrial action that constitutes the fundamental problem of labourism but rather a commitment to parliamentary representation without any specification of the content of that representation. As such, this book will have little to say about the 'class struggle' outside parliament.

Nairn's concentration on 'anti-intellectualism' and the influence of Victorian trade unionism is of crucial importance. Like Foote, he stresses the idea of the party as the *extension* of trade union thought and activity and criticizes this as totally inadequate for a political party. The few ideas, other than those relating to trade unionism, came from the Fabians and the ILP, and he characterizes these as weak. Nairn is overly harsh on the ideas of the ILP – their thinking ranged from religious non-conformity through elements of utopian socialism to Marxism. While the party did not embrace any of these as a whole, it incorporated them into its thought. In this sense the ILP was an ideological 'broad church' and Nairn does not acknowledge the potential strength of this. While he is right to stress the anti-intellectualism of the party, this is only part of a much wider problem of the anti-intellectualism of the nation. Although important, his characterization of labourism is therefore partial. Desai, concentrating exclusively as she does on the 'anti-intellectualism' of labourism, does not attempt to provide a holistic characterization, or rather she uses the term exclusively to denote this anti-intellectualism.

Saville's conception is also partial in that it concentrates on labourism as a 'bridge' between the bourgeois thinking of the nineteenth century and the labour movement. His suggestion that labourism is, in some sense, 'rooted' deeply in English traditions of thought which ultimately are antipathetic to socialist ideas is both unconvincing and profoundly conservative. Additionally, he has little to say on the labourism of the Labour Party in the twentieth century.

It will be obvious that this book, with its conception of labourism as the thoughts and activities of the Labour Party, will take issue with Marriott's ideas of it as predominantly related to working class *culture*. While his book is both interesting and very convincing, he is actually working with a completely different conception of the term to the one adopted here.

Thompson's 'authoritarian impulse', while also very interesting, does not, in itself, represent a defining characteristic of labourism. Nor does the party's embrace of the 'fantasy' of 'little England' that Elliott points to. Again, like Desai, he is not concerned to provide a comprehensive characterization of labourism.

However, the aim of this book is to arrive at such a characterization, one that will address the question of the party's effectiveness, and in the conclusion to this chapter I will provide an outline.

Conclusion – an 'outline' characterization of labourism

First, underlying everything else, there is a complete absence, right throughout the party's history, of a clear ideology. Actually, the very concept of 'ideology' has become extremely contentious in recent times and has been subjected to many negative connotations. However, to avoid being distracted from the main purpose of this chapter by a discussion of the nature of ideology and its potentially pejorative associations, a dictionary definition of '…the system of ideas at the basis of an economic or political theory…'[60] will be accepted and employed. Within the Labour Party, radical liberalism has had an important influence and 'trade union ideology' has clearly been central. Fabianism has had the most enduring, and therefore perhaps the most important, ideological influence on the Labour Party but, unsurprisingly, is itself vague. Undoubtedly the most important ideological influence that Fabianism has had is as regards its concentration on cautiousness and 'gradualism'.

The influence of socialist thought, from the left of the party, has been present since the beginning and has 'waxed and waned' throughout. However, it has been a relatively peripheral influence on the party's ideology and has been subject to the same 'logic of labourism' that has influenced the thinking of the party's right-wing and centre, as a number of commentators have pointed out, including Nairn, Thompson and Desai. The late 1970s and early 1980s represented a period of unprecedented strength of the left, and one which seems unlikely to be repeated.

Overall though, Labour has been less of an ideological 'broad church' and more of a vague, unprincipled, and pragmatic party. The vagueness of purpose that Miliband and others have drawn attention to is absolutely central and informs the party's confused approach to policy-making – the second characteristic of labourism presented here. The party was created, in 1900, without any aims other than parliamentary representation of working people and this has remained the case right throughout its history. It is as difficult to state the basic principles of the current Labour Party as it was those of the Labour Representation Committee in 1900.

The party's only clear overall aim is to achieve success in elections. Thus it could be said to be an embodiment of electoralism. The aim of achieving electoral representation has never been properly and adequately supported by an elaboration of the content of that representation. What is the Labour Party for? What does it hope to achieve? These questions *do* pose problems, even as regards the Labour Party's avowed aim of achieving electoral success, which has been achieved either through presenting a clear programme to the electorate or in particular historical circumstances. An example of the latter is the election of Labour in 1945 and an example of electoral success achieved through clarity of presentation is the election of Mrs Thatcher's government in 1979. Tony Blair's electoral success in 1997 had elements of both. First, the very limited aims of the party's election manifesto were clear and understandable. However, of much greater importance were the 'time for a change', Tory divisions and 'sleaze' factors. New Labour was the beneficiary of a combination of the electorate's boredom with the Conservatives after eighteen years in office and the perception of them, strongly fuelled by the media, as divided, corrupt and morally bankrupt. Labour did not so much persuade the electorate to vote *for* them as receive the votes of an electorate that simply had had enough of the Tories.

Without a clear ideology, policy formulation has much to do with the vagaries of the day, either as regards the electorate or the Labour leadership or both. Thus policy formulation is a piecemeal and reactive process. This issue is not new to New Labour. It has existed for as long as the Labour Party has existed: what is the Labour Party for and what does it hope to achieve once it is in government?

Third, this absence of ideology and confused approach to policy-making has meant that the party has always prioritised pragmatism over principles. Foote (1997) pointed out that Labour has always believed that it is more important to deal with specific problems rather than attempt to provide a comprehensive programme that would try to deal with these problems at source. The influence of Fabianism is crucial here with its emphasis on piecemeal gradualism.

Fourth, the contradiction of Labour's leaders always presenting it as a party of and in the *national* interest, in spite of it being a party that is organically linked to the trade unions, and therefore to a sectional interest. This, again, is true of the party's whole history. If Blair and his cohorts are successful in breaking or fundamentally weakening the link between the party and unions, it is highly likely that there will be a split in the party. However, this is mere speculation and is unlikely to occur. For the moment the trade unions and the Labour Party are as inextricably linked as they always have been. The discussion on the links with the trade unions could actually be said to be part of this contradiction of the party presenting itself as 'national'. If Blair publicly distances himself from the unions, the belief is that this will appeal to 'the nation'. However, it was noticeable that New Labour was keen to employ the undemocratic trade union 'block-vote' in support of their candidate in the election of the leader of the Welsh Labour Party in February 1999, an action that eventually backfired.

Fifth, throughout its history the party has been successful with its emotional appeal to both the electorate and its own members, through its rhetoric and, at times, policies on inequality and injustice. The party has always been perceived as a party of redistribution of wealth and is still perceived as such today, even though Stephen Byers prioritized *creation* of wealth over its redistribution in February 1999, and Gordon Brown resolutely refuses to use the term 'redistribution of wealth'. This emotional appeal has rarely been matched with policies or actions which address inequalities. However, the electorate, as well as many party members, have believed and continue to believe that this is the case: that the Labour Party is the party of redistribution, fairness, rights for workers and generally of social justice. The failure of the last Labour government to deliver on these promises has temporarily been forgotten. However, in 2001 the 'collective memory' of the electorate is already beginning to recall past events and link them to the current government, despite Blair's attempts to distance himself from the party's past by adding the prefix 'new' to its name.

Sixth, all of the above points contribute, in various ways, towards the party ultimately being *undemocratic*. Despite its apparently comprehensive democratic structures, the Labour Party has always been one in which the leader has wielded an enormous amount of power. Time and time again, party leaders, in government and in opposition, have either ignored or, at very best, diluted the policies of the party. Thus the party is undeniably 'top-down' in its structure and allows for little participation of the ordinary membership. The concept of democracy employed here is not one of direct or even necessarily 'participatory' democracy. Instead, it is merely related to the ability of the ordinary member, through the structures of the party, to affect and be involved in the formulation of policies. While extensive structures exist, supposedly to facilitate this, the party leadership often contradicts policy decisions that have been made using these structures. The complexities of the constitutional changes of *Partnership in Power* of 1997 will be examined in detail in the concluding chapter. The problems of a party that virtually ignores the democratic decisions of its own members and appeals directly to the electorate on the basis of vague and incoherent ideas will also be discussed in later chapters.

Seventh, the ineffectiveness of the party is directly bound up with its 'culture of defeatism', which is a key characteristic of labourism being presented here. The party has almost always followed the whims of the electorate on particular policy issues rather than seeing itself as a force for educational and hegemonic change. It has passively accepted the prejudices and ignorance of the electorate rather than attempting to change them. Thus, the relatively recent concern with single parents and with asylum seekers have appealed to people's worst tendencies to scapegoat sections of the population rather than made any attempt to change attitudes. This, in turn, is bound up with internal notions of what is 'realistic' as regards what the party can achieve. Any notion of the party having a hegemonic role is non-existent.

These seven points contribute to an overall characterization that is intended to address the question of the ineffectiveness of the party, *on its own terms*. That is, if we accept the aims and objectives of the party, an evaluation of its success will be made, measured against those very aims and objectives.

There is also the very important question, so far unaddressed, of whether or not labourism is an adequate and appropriate concept for understanding the various, and at times competing, ideologies and political practices that exist within the party. For example, can 'New Labour' be explained by reference to the concept of labourism? Is it a reaction and response to old-style labourism or is it merely labourism 'dressed up' in new, modernized clothes? This book will argue that labourism is an adequate and appropriate concept with which to characterize the Labour Party, including New Labour, for the whole of its history.

There is also the wider question of the extent to which the Labour Party is merely the British manifestation of a phenomenon that can be labelled 'Western European Social Democracy', but there is insufficient space to do justice to this question here. Is British labourism our national version of a wider form of social democracy or is there something peculiar to labourism that sets it apart? The question itself assumes a large amount of homogeneity between the social democratic parties of Western Europe and, while the differences between these parties are many and varied, there is a case for arguing for the relative homogeneity of Western European social democracy where the parties' origins, ideologies and historical trajectories are concerned. Many commentators treat the parties of Western Europe in this way, including Paterson and

Thomas (1977) (1986), Przeworski and Sprague (1986), Padgett and Paterson (1991), Scharpf (1991), Anderson and Camiller (1994) and a number of others.

I believe that that there are sufficient grounds for concluding that British labourism is different from its Western European counterparts. For example, the Labour Party was created by an alliance between the socialist societies, of which the ILP was the most important, and the trade unions. This level of trade union influence at its inception in itself marks it out as distinct from the Western European social democratic tradition. Another example is the almost complete absence of the influence of Marxism in the Labour Party, in theory and in practice, which makes it almost unique among West European parties. The absence of a clear ideology and the subsequent emphasis on pragmatism also mark it out as distinct.

The direct influence of Western European social democratic ideology and practice upon British labourism has also not been examined here. In fact, it has been minimal throughout the British party's history. The party has very rarely referred to itself as a social democratic party, preferring instead labels that have originated from within the British movement such as 'the party of social justice'. In this sense it has been very insular and somewhat nationalistic. Even Blair, while he is very keen to celebrate the pro-European stance of the current Labour Party, cites the British tradition as providing his values and principles rather than any influences from Western Europe. In fact his book, *New Britain: My Vision of a Young Country* (1996), makes only one very brief reference to 'European social democracy'. There are no other references to the concept of social democracy but at least nineteen to social justice.

Thus there are specificities of British labourism, as regards ideology, principles, policies, actions and experiences, both in terms of its own history and the Western European social democratic context, that can be evaluated as such. It is to this history that we will now turn.

Chapter 2
A short history of the British Labour Party

This chapter will present a history of the British Labour Party and will include a detailed examination of its aims and objectives. The Labour Party came into existence, as the Labour Representation Committee (LRC), in February 1900. However, it is obviously not possible to provide an exhaustive 101 year history in just one chapter. Instead, selective ideas, policies, actions and events will be examined for their particular relevance to the concept of labourism that is advanced in this book. Importantly though, they will be interwoven with an examination, and some evaluation, of Labour's stated aims throughout the century. History is always a selective process and this chapter adopts an unapologetically selective approach.

Events leading up to the formation of the Labour Representation Committee

First, a brief look at the events of the period leading up to the formation of the LRC in 1900. These have been well documented by Pelling (1965) and others. For our purposes it is worth briefly examining these events with particular regard to the formation of the ILP, the nature of the Fabian Society at the time and the influence of the SDF (Social Democratic Federation). We will also consider the nature of the trade union movement in the last two decades of the nineteenth century, particularly the relationship between the old skilled craft unions and the new unskilled unions and the relative influence of each in the formation of the LRC.

The ILP started its life in January 1893 in Bradford. It was felt at the time that the labour movement was becoming too large and unwieldy for the existing structures to cope. 'New unionism' was also making its presence felt, more of which later. The SDF was considered to be too revolutionary and the Fabians too close to the Liberal Party to represent the aspirations of the movement. The Fabian Society was also London-based, which aroused a great deal of suspicion and mistrust amongst Northern working-class socialists and 'labourists'. However, having said all this, the event that actually launched the creation of the ILP was a conference of Fabian societies held in London in 1892. The working-class Fabians from the north of England present at this meeting were absolutely convinced of the need for a new party. The London, predominantly middle-class, Fabians were not and most of them remained in the Fabian Society.

In line with Keir Hardie's proposals, the structure of the new party was based on the model of the Trades Union Congress (TUC), with a National Executive having the responsibility to carry out the decisions of conference. Hardie was also extremely influential in that he insisted upon the concept of *independent* labour representation in parliament, something he had personally practiced in his role as MP for West Ham since 1892. At its inaugural conference there was a proposal to name the new party the 'Socialist Labour Party' but this was rejected, after some discussion, because it was felt that the word 'socialist' might deter sections of the electorate from supporting it, and because it did not reflect all the party's roots, some of which were not explicitly socialist. The primary purpose of the new body was said to be to create a parliamentary party and it sought the trade unions, rather than the small socialist societies, as its allies. Pelling (1965) writes: 'In this decision the fundamental difference between the ILP and the earlier Socialist societies is revealed: the means of political action are regarded as of primary importance, and the theoretical approach gives way to the practical.'[61] This illustrates something of the foundations of labourism – the means were given priority over the ends. Admittedly, in the case of the ILP, a proposal clearly defining the object of the party was passed, which was not the case at the formation of the LRC seven years later. The object was said to be '..."to secure the collective ownership of the means of production, distribution and exchange"...'[62], a very familiar phrase which was to reappear, as the key part of the famous Clause Four of the Labour Party's constitution, a quarter of a century later.

The ILP also passed a programme which included restricting the working day to eight hours, the abolition of overtime, the prohibition of the employment of children under fourteen, provision for the sick, disabled, elderly, widowed and orphaned, free primary, secondary and university education, remunerated work for the unemployed, abolition of indirect taxation and a graduated income tax. While this may fall short of the socialist programme that Pelling describes it as, it is clearly a radical programme, and one which was not incorporated into the programme of the LRC.

The SDF declined to affiliate to the ILP (as did the London Fabian Society, for very different reasons) and criticized the decision not to include the word 'socialist' in the party's name. They suggested that this doomed the party's aims of 'emancipation of the workers' to failure. A similar argument was to be re-run seven and eight years later with the SDF's involvement in, and subsequent resignation from, the LRC.

As regards the founding of the LRC, the ILP was clearly the most influential group. In fact, without the ILP the LRC might never have come into existence. They were the main supporters and promoters of the idea of independent labour representation in Parliament and none was more passionate in their belief in this than Keir Hardie. Hardie's role in the creation of the LRC cannot be overestimated: he played an essential part in its inception. As for the various ideologies that found a place within the ILP, these ranged from non-conformist religious beliefs, through utopian socialism, to Marxism and much else besides. The ILP was the original Labour 'broad church' as regards the political views of its members.

The Fabian Society was created in 1884. Its very inception points to a characterization of its nature. Pelling (1965) writes: 'It sprang from a slightly older society called the Fellowship of the New Life, a vaguely Ruskinian, vaguely Owenite ethical society...'[63] It seems reasonable then to suggest that, at least at its beginnings, the Fabian Society was vague in both its philosophy and its aims. Indeed, Pelling (1965) comments that '...it is difficult to determine what the views of the original Fabians were.'[64] However, Edward Pease (1963), one of the founders of the Fabian Society, provides us with a declared aim: 'The Fabian Society was founded for the purpose of "reconstructing society" based on the competitive system, "in such manner as to secure the general welfare and happiness"'.[65]

The term 'Fabian' comes from Quintus Fabius Maximus. On this, the dictionary is useful: 'Pertaining to, or after the manner of, Q. Fabius

Maximus, surnamed Cunctator ('Delayer') from the tactics which he employed against Hannibal in the Second Punic War, and which consisted in avoiding a battle, and weakening the enemy by cutting off supplies and by continual skirmishing.'[66] Frank Podmore, who proposed the use of the name, wrote: 'For the right moment you must wait, as Fabius did most patiently, when warring against Hannibal, though many censured his delays; but when the time comes you must strike hard, as Fabius did, or your waiting will be in vain, and fruitless.'[67] In practice, however, Fabians have always emphasized caution and 'gradualism' and have prioritized this over 'striking hard'. Ironically, Fabius never did strike hard against Hannibal (Podmore was mistaken on this) and, true to their name, the Fabians have never done so either.

Pelling describes the Fabian Society's eccentric membership at its beginning and indicates that, at the time, it could not be taken seriously as a political organization. He quotes George Bernard Shaw: 'They had one elderly retired workman. They had two psychical researchers, Edward Pease and Frank Podmore, for whom I slept in a haunted house in Clapham. There were Anarchists, led by Mrs Wilson, who would not hear of anything Parliamentary. There were young ladies on the look-out for husbands, who left when they succeeded. There was Bland's very attractive wife Edith Nesbit, who wrote verses in the *Weekly Dispatch* for half a guinea a week, and upset all the meetings by making scenes and pretending to faint. She became famous as a writer of fairy tales...'[68]

Given these inauspicious beginnings, it does seem somewhat ironic (or perhaps not) that this organization has become the most ideologically influential within the Labour Party, and the most enduring, performing a very important task throughout the party's history. As we shall see, the Fabian Society was very important to the thinking of 'New Labour' in the second half of the 1990s.

The Fabians developed in an eclectic fashion, with elements of anarchism and Marxism having some influence in its early years. However, perhaps the single most influential member, Sidney Webb, was yet to join. George Bernard Shaw, who was his friend, introduced him to the Society in 1885, at a time when he was urging the middle classes to join. Webb was a senior civil servant. Along with a number of other new, middle-class recruits, he developed a distinctive political direction for the Society, suggesting that 'socialism' was implicit within capitalist society, and that inevitably and gradually society was evolving in this direction.

Thus, Webb wrote of the gains for socialism being made by the state control of '...dairies, milk-shops, bakeries, baby-farms, gasometers, schools of anatomy, vivisection laboratories, explosive works, Scotch herrings and common lodging-houses...'[69] This view of society was influenced by the thought of Eduard Bernstein, who was later to publish *Evolutionary Socialism*. The main issue for the Fabians, given the inevitability of socialism, was how to convince men, particularly those of influence, of the truth of its cause. Hence they published numerous 'fact-finding' pamphlets. They were strongly opposed to creating a new independent socialist, or even labour, party: they preferred 'permeation' of the two main political parties, particularly the Liberals. This belief continued well beyond 1900, and the presence of one representative of the Fabian Society on the LRC was a token gesture as they did not at that point support independent labour representation.

Even the Social Democratic Federation did not start life as an organisation based on socialist principles. Instead, in opposition to liberalism, it set itself up in 1881 as the Democratic Federation, as a radical rather than a socialist organisation. However, two years later, after driving out most of the radicals from its numbers, its leader, H.M. Hyndman, was able to convert it to an idiosyncratic version of socialism. In 1884 it became the Social Democratic Federation. Eleanor Marx joined, as did Tom Mann, John Burns and William Morris. The Federation preached socialist revolution but Hyndman's eccentric and autocratic leadership almost guaranteed failure. Nevertheless, it had some influence in the labour movement of the latter part of the century, particularly in Lancashire and London. Its role in the inception of the LRC will be examined later.

The trade unions were the other main component group of the LRC. It was the Amalgamated Society of Railway Servants that originally proposed, at the Trades Union Congress of 1899, a special conference of trade unions, co-operative and socialist societies to plan for independent labour representation in Parliament. The proposal came from Thomas Steels of the Doncaster branch of the union, who was an ILP member. The extent to which the formation of the LRC could be said to have originated from the trade unions is debatable. It is thought that the resolution was drafted by the ILP leaders in London and moved by Steels. It reads: 'That this Congress, having regard to its decisions in former years, and with a view to securing a better representation of the interests of labour in the House of Commons, hereby instructs the Parliamentary Committee to invite the co-operation of all the co-operative, socialistic, trade-union, and other working organisations to jointly co-operate on lines mutually agreed upon, in convening a special congress of representatives from such of the above-named organisations as may be willing to take part to devise ways and means for securing the return of an increased number of labour members to the next Parliament.'[70]

It appears from this resolution that the ILP did not, at this time, intend to set up an organisation with a long term aim: they refer to 'the next Parliament'. This has led Pelling (1982) to speculate that the formation of the LRC in 1900 was comparable to the founding of other labour representation organisations such as the Labour Representation League in 1869 and the Labour Electoral Committee in 1886. It is indeed fascinating to consider the possibility that the ILP, the TUC and other bodies intended nothing more than a short-term electoral arrangement to try to secure increased labour representation 'to the next Parliament'. This would go some way to explaining the vague, pragmatic and somewhat opportunistic aim for the organisation that Hardie proposed at the 1900 conference. It is possible that the organisation that became the Labour Party was merely intended as a short-term electoral arrangement between the various bodies involved, and no thought was given at the time to the longer term. However, this remains mere speculation.

It appears that the main trade unions supporting Steels' 1899 resolution, were the new unions of unskilled workers whose very existence was insecure. They hoped that parliamentary representation would remedy this situation. Interestingly, though, the resolution was only narrowly carried, with 546,000 votes in favour and 434,000 against.

Ross McKibbin (1974) suggests that the new, unskilled unions were strongly influenced by socialism while the older craft unions were more closely allied to radical Liberalism. This 'new unionism' was based on the unskilled industries and received an important symbolic boost from the Great Dock Strike of 1889 by the London dockers. This is often cited as the main stimulus to the new form of trade unionism. From 1890 to 1893 there were dockers strikes at nearly all the major ports to try to enforce 'closed shops'. They were all defeated but the new unionism itself was not. In transport and in gas, electricity and water, it continued to thrive. During the 1890s many of the new unions managed to achieve some of the rights and recognition of the 'old' unions, and therefore the distinction between the two began to blur, particularly as the employer's counterattack affected both equally. Even though the success of new unionism was small, its political success was perceived to be great. Ben Tillet, one of the leaders of the dockers union, wrote: 'It marked...the beginning of the close alliance in thought and purpose between the Trade Union Movement and the Socialist Movement which produced in due time the Labour Party.' [71]

John Saville (1988) argues that in the late nineteenth and early twentieth centuries labourism was primarily an ideology of the skilled workman. In contrast, Pelling (1982) suggests that the main supporters of the creation of the LRC, at the TUC conference which first suggested its formation, were '...the leaders of the new unskilled unions, who evidently hoped that parliamentary representation would be a valuable safeguard of the future existence of their organisations.' [72] Looking at the ideological inclinations of different types of workers in Sheffield in the early twentieth century, Chris Wrigley (Brown 1985) concludes that those in the new heavy industries were more likely to be socialists while those in the older light crafts were more likely to be Liberal radicals. Pelling (1965) writes: '...even at the end of the century the great majority of trade-union *leaders* [my italics] were members of the Liberal Party, and Gladstonians at that.' [73] Add Miliband's comments that most of the trade unionists at the LRC's founding conference were radical Liberals and the picture, as regards ideological orientation, becomes somewhat confusing. However, it is sufficient to note here the enormous influence of Liberalism, probably mostly of the radical variety, on the founding of what later became the Labour Party.

The creation of the LRC

On the 27th and 28th February 1900 the LRC was set up with the aim of establishing '...a distinct Labour group in Parliament, who shall have their own Whips, and agree upon their policy, which must embrace a readiness to co-operate with any party which for the time being may be engaged in promoting legislation in the direct interests of labour, and be equally ready to associate themselves with any party in opposing measures having an opposite tendency...' [74] This aim was proposed to the 1900 conference in the form of an amendment by Keir Hardie opposing an attempt by the SDF to get the conference to support the formation of '...a distinct party, with a party organisation separate from the capitalist parties based upon a recognition of the class war...[75] [and] the socialisation of the means of production, distribution and exchange.'[76] It could be argued, then, that the basic aim of the LRC was itself formed in opposition to socialist ideas, since the SDF resolution was explicitly socialist in content while Hardie's was obviously not.

The other aim agreed at the conference was '...working-class opinion being represented in the House of Commons by men sympathetic with the aims and demands of the Labour movements, and whose candidature are promoted by one or other of the organised movements represented at this Conference.'[77] A Mr T. Aspinwall of the Miners' Federation proposed that the conference should '...lay down the programme of the party before deciding as to candidatures,'[78] but his words went unheeded. As Miliband (1972) and others have noted, the aims and demands of the labour movements were left undefined. This issue is of crucial importance to the notion of labourism being advanced here in this book.

It is also very interesting, and important, to note that some of the wording of the SDF resolution appeared in the first LRC manifesto for the general election of 1900. After listing a number of radical measures the manifesto concludes: 'The object of these measures is to enable the people ultimately to obtain the Socialisation of the Means of Production, Distribution and Exchange, to be controlled by a Democratic State in the interests of the entire Community, and the Complete Emancipation of Labour from the Domination of Capitalism and Landlordism, with the Establishment of Social and Economic Equality between the Sexes.'[79] Never again does such a radical overall aim appear in a Labour manifesto, or any other Labour literature for that matter. It is worth remembering that at this point the SDF were still involved in the LRC and it is possible that they managed to get this inserted into the manifesto. Nevertheless, its inclusion is somewhat remarkable and little commented upon in the literature on the early Labour Party.

This clear statement of socialist intent represents an unprecedented and unrepeated event. It might be suggested that the inclusion of Clause Four in the party's constitution in 1918 is comparable but the wording of Clause Four is not as explicit and precise as this statement in the 1900 manifesto. This issue will be examined later in the chapter. So, given that the statement above is unique, how did it get to be there? The influence of Marxism and socialist thought is evident, so why was it included, given that the conference which had created the LRC had rejected the SDF resolution in favour of Hardie's much vaguer proposal? As already stated, the presence of the SDF in the LRC, plus the very strong influence of the ILP at the time, may have had some effect. The wording, as regards the socialisation of the means of production, distribution and exchange, is identical to the SDF resolution that was rejected at the inaugural conference. Perhaps the ILP agreed to its inclusion in the manifesto as a sop to the LRC after being instrumental in its rejection from the party's aims? Interestingly, by 1910, in the manifesto for the general election of that year, the familiar Labour rhetoric had replaced this explicit commitment. The manifesto concluded: 'Vote for the Labour candidates. The land for the people. The wealth for the wealth producers. Down with privilege. Up with the people.'[80] However, the 1900 statement was clearly an isolated aim and had very little bearing and influence on the conduct of the LRC's representatives in Parliament.

Ross McKibbin (1974) draws our attention to a fundamental difference between the ILP and the organisation that it was responsible for creating: 'Whereas the ILP had a more or less coherent critique of capitalism, corporatively the Labour Party had none. The reasons for its establishment were more prudential.'[81] This prudence relates to the inability of the Liberal Party at the time to represent working-class interests and oppose imperialism. He writes '…the conference which met at the Memorial Hall, Farringdon Street, in February 1900, was agreed upon independent Labour representation, but upon little else. It was assumed that the new party would defend the 'interests' of the working class in parliament and protect the threatened privileges of the unions, but it had no 'objective' other than the negative one that it renounced support for all other parties.'[82]

As already stated, this is an absolutely crucial aspect of the characterization of labourism being advanced in this book: the Labour Party started its life without any aim other than parliamentary representation of 'working-class opinion'. Trade union support, therefore, in the absence of any specific aims and objectives, translated into incorporation of trade union principles and methods of organisation. Radical Liberalism found its way in as an ideology and the negotiation and compromise tactics of the trade unions became 'operational norms'. Also, the party mirrored the organisational structure of the unions, with a central body that was much more powerful than its regional and local 'satellites'. This was so much the case that the introduction of the new constitution in 1918, with a network of constituency parties, at first made very little difference. The party's inextricable link with the unions continues to be of primary importance, right through to the present day, as a characteristic of labourism.

There is no doubt whatsoever that the infamous Taff Vale judgment of 1901 gave enormous impetus to the Labour Party and provided the foundation for its trade union base. The Taff Vale railway company took the union, the Railway Servants, to court over the issue of a strike and damaged company property. The company won and the decision was confirmed by the House of Lords in 1902. Even though the dispute began with a local official acting on his own initiative, the union was ordered to pay £23,000. Trade unions realized that they were susceptible to similar action being taken against them and so support for parliamentary representation to combat such things as the Taff Vale decision became the logical and inevitable next step. During 1901-2 the number of industrial bodies affiliated to the committee rose from 65 to 127. In 1902 individual members of trade unions affiliated to the committee was only 455,450 out of a total of 2 million trade union members nationally. However by 1903 this had risen to 847,000 and by 1904 to 956,000. In just two years, the numbers of trade union members more than doubled. Much of this was obviously due to the Taff Vale judgment. Trade unions affiliated, in large numbers, to the Labour Party, not because they believed in the positive aims and objectives that it advanced, but rather for the 'defensive' reason of trying to get support for getting rid of this particular law. L.T. Hobhouse accurately noted: 'That which no Socialist writer or platform orator could achieve was effected by the judges.'[83]

Whilst trade unions were flocking to join the LRC, the SDF left it, in disgust, in 1901 after the conference of that year failed to adopt their proposal to recognise '…the class war as the basis of working-class political action.'[84]

There was a notable lack of electoral support in the early years of the party. The highest proportion of the vote it received in all of the general elections before 1914 was 7.6 per cent of the electorate. K.D. Brown (1985) attributes this lack of support '…partly to the party's failure to produce much in the way of a distinctive political programme…'[85] He goes on to write: 'Generally, Labour was unable to produce policies identifiably its own, and this was the direct consequence of the circumstances in which the party was founded. It was devised primarily as a vehicle for working class representation, not as a machine for the implementation of a particular political creed or a specific set of policies.'[86]

The change of name in 1906

After the 1906 general election the thirty MPs who had been elected under the banner of the LRC changed themselves into the Labour Party. Importantly, at this stage it was a parliamentary party. That is, the organisation that changed its name was still essentially a parliamentary representation committee. It did not have an extensive national network of members and supporters – something which is usually considered to be an essential element of a political party. That was to come much later, the process beginning in 1918. Therefore the development of the Labour Party as a national political party was clearly from the top down. For the moment this will be merely noted since our immediate concern is with the events of 1906 onwards – a period when, despite its new title, the Labour Party was still a parliamentary representation group.

Of the thirty Labour MPs elected in 1906, twenty-two were supported by their trade unions and eight by the ILP. Eleven of those sponsored by unions were also ILP members. Most of them were middle-aged and had first come to politics as radical Liberals. Three of the most prominent – Keir Hardie, Arthur Henderson and David Shackleton – had been senior activists in the Liberal Party. Also, in twenty-four of the thirty constituencies that had returned a Labour MP, it was as a direct result of an electoral agreement that had been made between MacDonald and Gladstone, then Liberal Chief Whip.

The thirty individual members of the parliamentary Labour Party had enormous influence to determine its direction and policy. Apart from the liberal ideological influence, which was considerable, their trade union backgrounds as negotiators tended them to favour compromise and the concept of limited improvement. Also, most supported the need for individual thrift and temperance, both of which had their roots in working-class radicalism. Religion, usually of the non-conformist variety, also had an influence. Given that the party had a very vague and limited overall aim, the ages and backgrounds of the individual MPs was of enormous importance. They were the first Labour Party and, provided that they stayed within the boundaries of parliamentary representation of 'working-class opinion', they had no other constraints on their thoughts and actions. That is, in the absence of an aim and a set of objectives, and therefore policies, and a national party outside parliament, the Labour members were free to do what they wanted, in the interests of representing working-class opinion. This, very importantly, established a precedent that became a tradition within the parliamentary Labour Party and had a wide degree of acceptance within the party as a whole, once it had become established. The relative autonomy of the Labour MP has become an accepted part of the *modus operandi* of the labour movement. However, importantly, this has not come about as a conscious or collective decision regarding the best method of operation of the party. Instead, it is merely an historical accident, as an indirect result of the party having no guiding aim at its inception.

The concern of this group of MPs with the 'right to work', as a result of their first-hand experience of unemployment, was one of the few issues that distinguished them from the Liberals. Again, their personal backgrounds were of enormous importance in determining the collective concern of this first ever Labour Party. As regards its ideology, David Martin (Brown 1985) writes: 'It combined the rhetoric of Victorian moral reform with newer slogans urging social and economic revolution. There were libertarian elements that drew on Shelley and Carpenter, and Fabian programmes based on bureaucratic control. To some members socialism was the equivalent within a society of biological evolution, to others it was neither scientific nor desirable. Secularists dedicated to an earthly paradise in the form of 'Merrie England' and the precept that 'fellowship is life' were part of the same movement as those who believed that the Labour Party incorporated the teachings of the Sermon on the Mount. Little regarding any intellectual contradictions, many individuals combined several strands of thought.'[87] With such diverse ideological influences, there is little surprise that the Labour Party was unable to agree on a clear aim at its inception. Thus the logic and operation of compromise was there at, and in, the very formation of the British Labour Party. It was not merely compromise as an 'operational norm' that was accepted but, crucially, the compromise between various, and at times competing, ideologies and types of thought that was incorporated into the very structure of the party.

According to Martin, who presents a positive view of this diversity, this means that the ideology of the party incorporates the values which come out of the experiences of the working class. This is, at the very least, debatable. Because the party has never been able to agree on an ideology, and consequently had a limited strategy of parliamentary representation without the content of that representation being specified, the result is often more of a muddle than a reflection of the diversity of the experiences of the working class.

Early opposition from within

As early as 1908 there were some criticisms of the shortcomings of the party. Ben Tillet, the radical dock workers' leader, published *Is the Parliamentary Party a Failure?* in that year. In it he called the parliamentary leaders '…sheer hypocrites' who 'for ten and five guineas a time will lie with the best…'[88] In 1907 Victor Grayson had been elected to Parliament as an independent socialist. He had not received the backing of the ILP or the Labour Party but was supported by his local ILP in Colne Valley. He sat as an independent member and was a fiery parliamentary performer, arguing passionately for the unemployed, which eventually led to his suspension from Parliament. Grayson's behaviour was an embarrassment to the Labour MPs who were at pains to appear as respectable as possible. He lost his seat in 1910 and immediately began campaigning for an end to the 'Labour Alliance'. This led, in 1911, to the formation (in combination with the SDF and a small number of ILP branches) of the British Socialist Party, which later became the Communist Party of Great Britain.

In 1910, four of the members of the ILP National Council published a pamphlet entitled *Let Us Reform the Labour Party*. It bitterly denounced most of the members of the parliamentary party for abandoning the original principles of the ILP and stated: '…Labour must fight for Socialism and its own hand against BOTH the Capitalist parties IMPARTIALLY.'[89] The leaders of the parliamentary party, including Hardie and MacDonald, did their best to defend themselves against these attacks. Hardie published *My Confession of Faith in the Labour Alliance* in 1910. However, even he was unhappy. He said: 'The Labour Party…had ceased to count: the Press ignored it; the Cabinet Ministers made concessions to the Tory Party and to the Irish, seemingly oblivious of the fact that there was a Labour Party in the House.'[90] Also, Philip Snowden in 1914 said: 'The present labour representation in parliament…is there mainly by the goodwill of the Liberals, and it will disappear when that goodwill is turned into active resentment.'[91]

Also in 1910, the party re-stated its aim to: '…secure the election of Candidates to Parliament and organize and maintain a Parliamentary Labour Party, with its own whips and policy.'[92] This continued the somewhat negative aim of 1900, which was essentially to differentiate itself from the Liberal Party. However, this is an electoral strategy rather than a political aim. If the aim of an organisation is to get elected to power, then what is the purpose of that power, other than to hold office for its own sake?

The new constitution of 1918

In 1918, at the end of the First World War, the Labour Party adopted a new constitution and set itself up as a party with a national network of constituency parties. As Paul Adelman (1972) comments: 'Henderson aimed at grafting on to the federal structure a nationwide network of local constituency parties.'[93] It is this 'grafting on', from the top down, a process of adding on to the central parliamentary organization, that represents Labour's process of democratization of the party. The process was one in which a centralized body attempted to form a national political party. There were already local affiliated bodies such as ILP branches and trades councils but these had to be 'moulded' and added to, to create a national structure. This creation of a national political party from the top down constitutes an aspect of its undemocratic nature: one of the characteristics of labourism that is being presented here.

For our purposes, the most important part of the new constitution is Clause Four, part four, the so-called 'socialist clause', which read – 'To secure for the producers by hand and brain the full fruits of their industry, and the most equitable distribution thereof that may be possible, upon the basis of the common ownership of the means of production and the best obtainable system of popular administration and control of each industry or service.'[94] The inclusion of, responses to and debates on Clause Four are some of the most important elements of the history of labourism. Why did the Labour Party adopt this clause? Is it really socialist? What does it mean? To what extent has the Labour Party put it into practice during the seventy-seven years of its existence?

On the left of the Labour Party, Clause Four was generally thought of as the 'socialist clause'. It was constantly cited as providing the basis for labour's socialist ideology. Tony Benn, in *Arguments for Socialism* (1980), wrote – 'It remains the clearest and best possible statement of the democratic, socialist faith…'[95] Ken Coates' *New Labour's Aims and Values, A Study in Ambiguity* is a good, recent example of a Labour Left response to the rewriting of Clause Four, referring to the '…explicitly socialist commitment…'[96] in the clause. These are just two examples of the left's belief in Clause Four as a statement of socialist intent. Contrast this with Tony Blair's view expressed in a Fabian pamphlet of 1995, *Let Us Face the Future*: '…the party established 'clear red water' between itself and the Liberals, in the form of clause IV of the party's constitution…but at the time Sidney Webb saw the 'socialist clause' as a fudge.'[97]

McKibbin (1974) asks the very important question of how this clause, the 'socialist objective' as he calls it, came to be included at all. He provides us with a number of reasons, starting with the need of the party to differentiate itself from the Liberals. It provided direction for the party's new programme and finally '…precisely because of its vagueness and lack of rigour paradoxically it had an umbrella function: it was an acceptable formula in a Party where there was otherwise little doctrinal agreement.'[98]

However, was Clause Four as vague and lacking in rigour as McKibbin suggests? In stating that common ownership of the means of production, and, later, distribution and exchange, was the party's aim, was it not making an explicit commitment to a form of socialism? Or is it the case, as Miliband (1972) suggests, that the commitment made was to *labourism* rather than to socialism? McKibbin states that the reason for the inclusion of Clause Four was: '…not because the working class had become socialist…but because an important section of the middle classes had.'[99] The latter were more important to the Fabians than were the working classes. He argues that jingoistic support for the First World War from trade unionists moved the party to the right and therefore Clause Four was '…inserted in a constitution that confirmed the triumph of the unions and the defeat of the socialists.'[100] The trade unionists were able to point, with legitimacy, to the middle-class origins of the socialists within the party.

Another important possible explanation is that Clause Four was inserted as a sop to the ILP because of the undermining of their power by the 1918 constitution. Prior to this, they were the main organization in the constituencies and individuals wishing to become members of the Labour Party had to first join either the ILP or the Fabian Society. Membership of one of the latter would automatically lead to membership of the former. The new constitution brought an end to this and, the argument goes, the ILP were 'compensated' for this erosion of power by the inclusion of Clause Four.

One very important question to ask here is whether or not Clause Four can be construed as a statement of *socialist* intent or if it can be interpreted in other ways. Does the common ownership of the means of production, distribution and exchange equate with socialism? Some commentators suggest that Clause Four could be said to be merely a statement regarding public ownership, but in my view it undoubtedly is a socialist statement. Common ownership of the means of production, distribution and exchange means exactly that. However, perhaps a better way to approach the problem is not to ask what the clause means, but rather to ask why it was included in the 1918 constitution. The authors of the constitution were Arthur Henderson and Sidney Webb. Tony Blair has said that the inclusion of Clause Four was a 'fudge'. G.D.H. Cole (1948) refers to it as '...a plainly Socialist declaration...'[101], whilst acknowledging that it avoids using the word 'socialism'. Ralph Miliband accepts that its inclusion meant that the party had rid itself of liberalism, but goes on to use the contents of *Labour and the New Social Order*, the statement of policy that accompanied it, as evidence that it had been replaced by labourism rather than socialism.

Because Clause Four itself is so short and basic, it is useful now to examine very briefly the content of *Labour and the New Social Order* for additional information. It was based on four principles: the concept of 'a national minimum', democratic control of industry (with very vague proposals); financial reform and surplus wealth to be used for the common good. The first of these included a commitment to full employment. The second really meant public ownership under the control of parliament. The third essentially meant introducing a progressive taxation system, and the last was about putting the concept of equality of opportunity into practice. It is widely accepted to be a document that was heavily influenced by Fabian thinking. As Miliband states: 'The full implementation of all of the proposals contained in Labour and the New Social Order would, of course, have left the bulk of the means of life in private hands, even though under some measure of State control.'[102] Thus, while Clause Four can be said to be a statement of socialist intent, the programme that accompanied it and provided substance for it was clearly not a socialist programme. Both Miliband and Blair, and others, agree that the main function of the clause was to establish a clear difference between the Labour Party and the Liberals; something it was very keen to do in its early years. However, was there any more to the inclusion of the clause than this? The short answer is that we will never actually know, but given that the writer of the clause was a leading member of the Fabian Society, it is unlikely that its inclusion was for explicitly socialist reasons.

The various debates on Clause Four that have taken place throughout the party's history have been extremely important in differentiating those on the left of the party who are explicitly socialist in their ideology and in their actions from the rest. While the latter can more easily be classified as labourist in their ideologies and approaches, it is my intention to include the Labour Left within this book's delineation of labourism. Tony Blair finally put paid to all debates on Clause Four by replacing it at a special conference in April 1995. The new Clause Four will be examined in the section on 'New Labour' at the end of this chapter.

McKibbin (1974) makes a very convincing argument which completely contradicts the view that the inclusion of Clause Four in the party's constitution meant that it had become a socialist party. He suggests that by 1919 the only vestige of socialism left in the party was in the Labour Research Department and that by 1924 this too had disappeared. He writes that, as a result of this – 'A Party with a socialist objective but no socialist ideology needs something else: the movement and service to the movement became a substitute.'[103] It seems that loyalty to this movement was the primary consideration, and principles came a very long way behind in importance.

The aims of the party in 1918 were remarkably similar to those of the Blair government in 1997 – the 'one nation' aspirations of a united country with economic opportunity for all. McKibbin concludes – 'If it is objected that it [the Labour Party] has not served the cause of socialism or even the 'true' interests of the working classes the answer is that it was never designed to do so.'[104] This point is as pertinent today as it was eighty-three years ago.

The first Labour government

In 1924, as a result of a series of remarkable events, the first Labour government took office. It was a minority government, Labour having 191 members, the Liberals 158 and the Tories 258. The Labour Party was therefore entirely dependent upon Liberal support. The election had been fought on Tariff Reform and both Labour and the Liberals had advocated Free Trade. Thus the Liberals were willing, reluctantly, to give their support to a Labour government. The leader of the Liberal Party, H. Asquith, told his parliamentary colleagues: '…if a Labour government is ever to be tried in this country, as it will be sooner or later, it could hardly be tried under safer conditions.'[105] Neville Chamberlain also thought that Labour '…would be too weak to do much harm but not too weak to get discredited.'[106]

Perhaps one of the most enlightening facts about this first ever Labour government was the formation of its strategy. This was carried out, at a private meeting at Sidney Webb's house, by just five men – MacDonald, Snowden, Thomas, Henderson and Webb. They decided, unsurprisingly, to pursue a cautious strategy rather than attempt to '…introduce some bold Socialist measures, knowing, of course, that we should be defeated upon them.'[107] This blatantly undemocratic behaviour, with these five men consulting no one about this strategy, set a precedent for future Labour cabinets, and one which they have been all too keen to follow. This constitutes another key aspect of the characterization of labourism being presented here.

1926 and 1931

The events of the General Strike of 1926 are very familiar to labour historians and observers. They will be examined very briefly here with reference to the relevance to the concept of labourism of the abandoning of the strike. The basic conflict was over the coal owners' decision, in 1925, to reduce the wages of miners. The Conservative government supported this decision. The miners union advocated militant resistance and received strong support from the trade union movement. After the threat of a coal strike, the government agreed to pay a subsidy to the industry until May 1st 1926 while undertaking an inquiry. However, they were adamant that the coal owners should not be prevented from reducing the miners' wages and made extensive preparations, mainly through the creation of the Organization for the Maintenance of

Supplies, for the possibility of a general strike. Labour, both party and unions, did not prepare properly. Divisions and outright opposition to a general strike prevented this. Nevertheless a date was set for the start of the strike – May 4th. The negotiating committee of the TUC General Council were desperate to avert it, but the government was steadfast, and the strike began at midnight on May 3rd. Almost from the beginning of the strike, negotiations had been resumed to bring it to an end. But despite massive support and involvement it was called off unconditionally by the General Council on May 12th.

Miliband (1972) writes of the ending of the General Strike – 'The Labour movement *was* betrayed, but not because the Labour leaders were villains or cowards. It was betrayed because betrayal was the inherent and inescapable consequence of their whole philosophy of politics – and it would be quite foolish to think that their philosophy was the less firmly held for being unsystematically articulated.'[108] This conception of 'betrayal', with which this book completely concurs, constitutes one of the main elements of what might be termed the 'logic of labourism'. That is, 'betrayal' was the operation, in practice, of a vague, unprincipled and undemocratic approach to the issue of political strategy. This represents a very important element of the argument being presented here, which will be returned to later.

MacDonald's 'great betrayal' of 1931 is equally familiar to those who study Labour's history and will not be examined here in any detail. The backdrop to it was the coming to office of the second Labour government in 1929, again dependent upon Liberal, and this time even Conservative, support. It seems that MacDonald found it much easier to negotiate with Liberals and Conservatives than the Labour left. The other aspect of its context was the huge rise in unemployment: to 2.8 million in July 1931. The economic situation worsened and cuts in unemployment benefit and teachers pay were proposed. Not surprisingly, the TUC General Council opposed these proposals and MacDonald offered his resignation to the King, who persuaded him, with support from both Conservative and Liberal leaders, to lead a National Government. Snowden, Thomas and Lord Sankey went with him and all were expelled from the Labour Party.

It is enough to note here that MacDonald's decision to lead a National Government shows that Labour leaders can, at the very least, become dissociated and disconnected from the movement and from the people they are supposed to represent. They often have more in common with the leaders of other political parties than they do with their own members. MacDonald's act can be characterized as a logical next step for a leader who had become detached from the rest of his party. It was rumoured before the general election of 1997 that Tony Blair was considering the possibility of including non-Labour Party MPs in his cabinet after the election. The names of Paddy Ashdown and Michael Heseltine were mentioned. While this did not happen, perhaps for obvious reasons, Blair did have a consultation meeting with Margaret Thatcher immediately after becoming Prime Minister. In July 1997, just two months after the election, he formed a cross-party cabinet committee with the Liberal Democrats to discuss common concerns, beginning with constitutional reform. He also appointed a number of businessmen to either government positions or advisory jobs, including Sir David Simon, the former Chairman of BP, who was appointed Minister for Trade and Competition in Europe, Martin Taylor, the Chief Executive of Barclays Bank, who was employed in an advisory role, and Geoffrey Robinson, the former Jaguar Chief Executive, who became the Paymaster General, despite having had no opposition front bench experience. Tory ex-Ministers were also given a role: Chris Patten was made the head of the inquiry into policing in Northern Ireland and David Mellor was made Head of the Football Task Force. Also, Lord Jenkins, the Liberal Democrat peer, was appointed to lead a commission looking at electoral reform. All of these point to a very high degree of autonomy for the Prime Minister himself.

All too often Labour's leaders have acted with almost absolute autonomy and with little accountability to the movement and the people that elected them into power. MacDonald's actions in 1931 were a step too far for the labour movement but the relative ease with which he was able to leave the Labour Party and movement behind, in order to lead a National Administration, suggests a very high degree of independence from that party and movement. The events of 1931 convinced the ILP to disaffiliate from the Labour Party, which they did in July 1932.

The post-war Labour governments
In 1945, the Labour Party went to the country with the manifesto *Let Us Face the Future*. It included sections on a commitment to full employ-

ment, 'socialisation' of key industries, economic controls (rationing), agriculture, a house-building programme, limited nationalisation of land, and world peace. On opening the debate on the programme which formed the basis for the manifesto at the party conference of 1945, Herbert Morrison (Peter Mandelson's grandfather), on behalf of the National Executive Committee, commented on the 'socialisation' proposals contained in it: 'In your speeches you must not only make a case against capitalist private enterprise, which is easy, but you must spend substantial time in arguing the case for the socialisation of these industries on the merits of their specific cases. That is how the British mind works. It does not work in a vacuum or in abstract theories.'[109] Morrison's comments and advice are very instructive in that they represent, in the starkest terms, the labourist approach to political strategy generally. Instead of attempting to persuade people of the merits of 'socialisation' of industry generally, candidates are urged to argue on the merits of specific cases. Thus, the thinking is that each industry in question will present merits to support the argument for nationalisation. This is an excellent example of the party's piecemeal approach referred to earlier, and very much represents the influence of Fabian thinking on the party's strategy.

Morrison also refers to the specificity of the programme and declares that all candidates should only make promises on the basis of it – a statement very similar to Tony Blair's commitments in the 1997 general election campaign and his exhortations to party candidates. Morrison's speech was generally warmly received by the 1945 conference. The one or two slightly critical comments concentrated on omissions in *Let Us Face the Future* such as mention of the fishing industry, Scotland and local government. The one general dissenting voice, a Mr Trevor Pugh of Westbury DLP, said: 'This document is not sufficient for the period in which we are living...We cannot see distinctly enough in this document that we are anything more than just another political party; we are a great movement of the common people, and this is an historic moment when the common people must take power into their hands.'[110]

Unsurprisingly, the Labour manifesto for the 1945 election concentrated on a prosperous peace after the war, full employment, public ownership of specific industries, agriculture, house-building, the land, education, health and social insurance. The two general statements that are made in the manifesto about overall aims are: 'The nation wants food, work and homes. It wants more than that – it wants food in plenty, useful work for all, and comfortable, labour-saving homes that take full advantage of the resources of modern science and productive industry. It wants a high and rising standard of living, security for all against a rainy day, an educational system that will give every boy and girl a chance to develop the best that is in them.'[111] And in the section on public ownership of industries: 'The Labour Party is a Socialist Party and proud of it. Its ultimate purpose at home is the establishment of the Socialist Commonwealth of Great Britain – free, democratic, efficient, progressive, public-spirited, its material resources organised in the service of the British people.'[112]

The 1945 election must be viewed within the context of public expectation after the Second World War. Fascism had been defeated and the British people had played a key role in this. Within Britain, as part of the war effort, women had gone out to work in munitions factories, there had been near full employment and people from different classes and sections of society had worked alongside each other in a common cause. The war effort and the defeat of Hitler had raised the expectations of the population enormously. Not only did they not want to return to the dark days of massive unemployment and grinding poverty of the 1930s, they felt that it was possible for Britain to rebuild itself and provide security and prosperity for *all* its people. Miliband (1973), Nairn (1964) and numerous others have drawn our attention to the radical spirit of the British people after the war and the high level of expectation of a bright new future.

So, was *Let Us Face the Future*, as Miliband suggests of its nationalization proposals, '…the least the Executive could present to the 1945 Conference without causing acute dissension in the Party.' ?[113] That is, was the programme and the subsequent manifesto the least that they could get away with? It does appear that after the war there was a tremendous mood for change amongst the British people. Importantly, this was not articulated as demands on the Labour Party to take socialist steps. However, the government could have gone much further as regards its 'socialization' measures, whether of industry or land, without much opposition. As Miliband has pointed out, the nationalization of industries that did take place had '…already been recommended, as Professor Brady has noted, "by Conservative dominated fact-finding and special investigating committees".'[114] This issue is absolutely crucial as regards the nature of this post-war government. It is now widely assumed that this Labour government transformed the economic and social base of Britain and, in a sense, it did. The creation in 1948 of the National Health Service and the system of social insurance supporting it were remarkable achievements which dramatically transformed the social life of the British people. However, as regards the issue of 'socialization' or nationalization of industry, the achievements are much less impressive. It seems that, with the exception of the iron and steel industry, which the Labour government procrastinated on anyway, all of the nationalization programmes that took place would probably have been carried out by a Conservative government. The government rescued these ailing industries rather than 'socialized' them and a Conservative government would, in the national economic interest, have almost certainly done exactly the same. So, Labour's aim, contained in its 1945 manifesto, of establishing a 'Socialist Commonwealth', was certainly not enacted in its public ownership measures.

Even the creation of the National Health Service and the system of Social Insurance underpinning it cannot be wholly credited to the 1945 government. The British Medical Association, as early as 1929, had proposed a national health service, and in 1944 the coalition government had produced a White Paper, based on the principles contained in the Beveridge Report of 1942. Admittedly all of these proposals would have fallen well short of the comprehensive and extensive service that Aneurin Bevan created in 1948. However, again, it seems highly likely that had the Conservative Party been elected to power in 1945, they also would have created a national health service.

The basic argument being presented here regarding the 1945 Labour government, is that it could have gone much further than it did with the 'socialization' of the economy, however one interprets that concept. If it is thought of as merely referring to public ownership of industries, the government could have done more, with greater speed and with less procrastination. If socialization of the economy is interpreted in a wider, socialist sense, again the Labour government of 1945 could have gone down that road, and received the support of the British population with very little opposition. So, in answer to the question of whether Labour's programme and manifesto of 1945 was the 'least that they could get away with', the answer is a very resounding 'yes'. This seems to be supported by the argument, advanced by Miliband and others, that by

1951 the government was completely exhausted of ideas and ready to stand aside to let the Conservative Party take its turn.

Gaitskell and Clause Four

Mention should be made very briefly of Hugh Gaitskell's attempts to revise Clause Four of the party's constitution in 1960. While the party conference of that year rejected his proposal, it did accept an additional statement of aims, which was said to reaffirm and clarify the party's objects. It included a statement that the party's '…social and economic objectives can be achieved only through an expansion of common ownership substantial enough to give the community power over the commanding heights of the economy'; and 'recognizing that both public and private enterprise have a place in the economy it believes that further extension of common ownership should be decided from time to time in the light of these objectives and according to circumstances, with due regard for the views of the workers and consumers concerned'.[115] The latter part of this statement clearly displays the influence of the Fabian 'piecemeal' approach. Overall, the statement dilutes the meaning of Clause Four so much as to render it ineffectual as a socialist clause. While many commentators look at Gaitskell's 'defeat' at the 1960 conference, few emphasize the importance of the acceptance of these additional aims or statement of principles.

Harold Wilson's technocracy

It was Harold Wilson who first introduced the labour movement to the idea of technocratic solutions to political problems. At the Labour Party Conference of 1963, he said: 'We are living perhaps in a more rapid revolution than some of us realize. The period of fifteen years from…1960 to the middle of the 1970s will embrace a period of technical change, particularly of industrial methods, greater than in the whole industrial revolution of the last 250 years…The problem is this…It is the choice between the blind imposition of technological advance, with all that means in terms of unemployment, and the conscious, planned, purposive use of scientific progress to provide undreamed of living standards and the possibility of leisure ultimately on an unbelievable scale…we are re-stating our Socialism in terms of the scientific revolution…The Britain that is going to be forged in the white heat of this revolution will be no place for restrictive practices or for outdated methods on either side of industry.'[116] Subsequent Labour leaders, most notably Neil Kinnock and Tony Blair, have embraced this technocratic approach to politics. Indeed, the party's manifesto of 1964 was entitled *The New Britain*, a theme continued in Blair's leadership and containing very similar sentiments about the role of industrial development, the need for 'flexibility' and, more generally, the need to 'modernize' Labour's approach to these issues. Wilson was wrong about the dates. The 'post-industrial revolution' is still happening today, but other than that his utterances thirty-seven years ago regarding Labour's role in it, are remarkably similar to Blair's in the late twentieth and early twenty-first centuries. David Coates (1975) writes: '...the Labour leadership went to the electorate in 1964 offering a technocratic vision of reality: of a world in which the structures of ownership and control need not prevent the exploitation of man's technological and scientific potential for the common good, and which had done so hitherto only because of the absence of purposive and persistent intervention and planning by a democratically responsive State.'[117]

While Wilson was the first Labour leader to express this in purely 'technocratic' terms, the novelty of his speech was really only in the notion of applying new technology to the resolution of political issues. Prior to this, Labour leaders, while not making explicit reference to technical change, were equally dismissive of the need to challenge 'structures of ownership and control'. The only thing that was different about Wilson's approach was his 'discovery' of new technology and industrial methods. This applies equally to Kinnock's 'modernization' and Blair's 'New Labour'. That is, Wilson, Kinnock and Blair represent continuity with the past, in their political approaches, rather than change and new directions. This is one of the fundamental points being made about the nature of labourism in this book: the Labour Party (and indeed movement) of Keir Hardie was essentially the same as the Labour Party (and movement) of Tony Blair. While there have been great changes in the last 101 years, some of which we have examined here, the labour movement has remained, as regards its dominant political strategy and approach to political problems, essentially unchanged for that whole period. Clearly this argument needs a lot of defending and most of this will take place in the concluding chapter.

However, there is an important point to be merely noted here and examined in greater depth later. Wilson's 'White Heat' speech was the first comprehensive response from a Labour leader to economic developments that will be termed here 'post-industrial'. This book's third chapter – a case study of the Sheffield labour movement – will examine labourism's response to and involvement in these developments, in an attempt to provide a recent illustration of the *modus operandi* of the labour movement.

The 1974 manifesto

In 1973, the Labour Party made another list of commitments in its Programme of that year. These found their way into the party manifesto for the election of February 1974. They were to – ' a. Bring about a fundamental and irreversible shift in the balance of power and wealth in favour of working people and their families; b. Eliminate poverty wherever it exists in Britain, and commit ourselves to a substantial increase in our contribution to fighting poverty abroad; c. Make power in industry genuinely accountable to the workers and the community at large; d. Achieve far greater economic equality – in income, wealth and living standards; e. Increase social equality by giving far greater importance to full employment, housing, education and social benefits; f. Improve the environment in which our people live and work and spend their leisure.'[118] These are indeed ambitious and laudable aims. However, I will argue that the very theory and practice of labourism actually prevented the achievement of these aims.

1983 and the response of the right

Gerald Kaufman called the Labour Party manifesto of 1983 '…the longest suicide note in history".'[119] The party put to the country a comprehensive statement of its aims. These were summarized by Michael Foot in the foreword to the document as: 'To get Britain back to work. To rebuild our shattered industries. To get rid of the ever-growing dole queues. To protect and enlarge our National Health Service and our other great social services. To help stop the nuclear arms race.'[120] The left-wing influence within the party in 1983 and the disastrous election result of that year have been widely accepted as 'proof' that socialist ideas are not, and never can be, popular with the British electorate. Tony Blair started his speech accepting the leadership of the party at the conference of 1994 with the words: 'I came into Parliament in 1983. Those were dark days…'[121] In response to this type of sentiment, the party has swung dramatically to the right, first with Kinnock's 'modern-ization' period and now with Blair's New Labour.

There is insufficient space in this chapter to fully examine this contention and the responses from the left. For the moment, it will merely be noted that the Labour Party as a whole has very rarely seen its role as an educational, 'hegemonic' one as regards public opinion on virtually any matter. Clearly, those on the left of the party were attempting to undertake this task in the late 1970s and early 1980s but the weight of the history of labourism (not to mention the right and the centre of the party) were clearly against them and their eventual defeat was inevitable. The response from the right and centre has been to return to the piecemeal politics of labourism. Blair has often spoken of his dislike of ideology, and the Labour election manifesto of 1997 was an exercise in 'piecemeal politics', with its specific remedies for specific prob-lems, something that Blair, incredibly, was able to celebrate as 'new' during the election campaign and ever since.

The incorporation of Keynesian economics and Beveridge 'welfarism', neither of which are social democratic in origin, into labourism after the Second World War set a precedent which made it possible for the labour movement, however contradictory it may seem, to incorporate elements of Thatcherism and monetarism into its thought and practice in the late 1980s and 1990s. Keynes's and Beveridge's ideas were no more intrinsi-cally social-democratic than those of monetarism. This very important, and somewhat contentious, point will only be noted here to illustrate the 'flexibility' of labourism. It will be pursued at length in the concluding chapter.

New Labour

It has already been stated that Fabianism has had a very strong influ-ence on the thinking of New Labour. The piecemeal and gradual approach is one manifestation of this. There is also a strong association between the Fabian Society and New Labour, with the former publishing the latter's most important pamphlets, and individuals within the party belonging to both, if indeed it can be said to be possible to belong to New Labour. In a Fabian pamphlet *Let Us Face the Future – the 1945 anniversary lecture* (1995), Tony Blair states: 'Our values do not change…The programme we are in the process of constructing entirely reflects our values. Its objectives would be instantly recognisable to our founders:..'[122] However, we should not just take Tony Blair's word for it. Let us compare his statements regarding his 'one-nation' approach to politics with Ramsay MacDonald's speech at the Royal Albert Hall in 1924, on the eve of the first Labour government, which was examined in the first chapter. The basic point being made is that New Labour does, as Blair acknowledges, represent a continuity with the past thinking of the Labour Party rather than a fundamental break with it. The only novel aspect of it (although this is not actually new, given that it has been a concern of Labour leaders since Harold Wilson) is the concentration on the aim '...to equip our country for massive economic and technological change;...'[123] Indeed, the second aim, in Blair's speech to the Fabian Society in 1995 – '...to provide jobs and security for all in this new world'[124] – simply repeats Wilson's exhortations, in his 'White Heat' speech of 1963, that the introduction of the new technology should be 'conscious, planned and purposive' rather than blindly imposed, to avoid mass unemployment.

This contrasts with claims of novelty made by Giddens (1998)[125] and Tony Wright (1997). The latter writes: 'What is distinctive about the New Labour project, which is why it terrifies the life out of the Conservatives, is that it is neither a return to old labourism nor an embrace of neo-liberalism. It offers a new synthesis – of market and state, public and private, individual and collective, rights and responsibilities – that opens up a distinctive political direction.'[126]

Blair's new Clause Four is an exercise in vagueness and rhetoric. It takes us right back to the vague aims at the inception of the party. Consider just its first point: 'The Labour Party is a democratic socialist party. It believes that by the strength of our common endeavour, we achieve more than we achieve alone so as to create for each of us the means to realise our true potential and for all of us a community in which power, wealth and opportunity are in the hands of the many not the few, where the rights we enjoy reflect the duties we owe, and where we live together, freely, in a spirit of solidarity, tolerance and respect.'[127] If this is compared to the clarity and forthrightness of the original Clause Four, it does indeed seem that Blair is attempting to obscure the meaning of Labour's aims and values. However it is a little clearer in the second point when it refers to the desirability of: '...a dynamic economy, serving the public interest, in which the enterprise of the market and the rigour of competition are joined with the forces of partnership and co-operation...'[128] This vague commitment to a 'mixed economy' could have been written at virtually any time during the 101 years of the party's history.

Overall, the new Clause Four lacks clarity, obscures the meaning of Labour's aims and values and ultimately presents a smokescreen for New Labour to carry on pursuing the undemocratic and piecemeal politics that the Labour Party has always pursued. The 'spin doctors' of New Labour are the direct political descendants of the five men who gathered in Sidney Webb's house in 1924 to decide the strategy of the first Labour government.

The New Labour government elected to power in May 1997 has also represented an exercise in the politics of piecemeal intervention. Its manifesto celebrated such an approach, as already examined, and its actions have been as 'pragmatic' and as selective as any other Labour government. The surprising aspect of this is that commentators and journalists are presenting its policies and actions as if they represent a new departure from 'Old Labour' politics. Whilst it is clearly the case that New Labour is somewhat to the right of the party of the 1970s and early 1980s, the latter was a temporary and brief movement to the left and, it is being argued throughout this book, was still within the boundaries of labourism. New Labour is merely a 'modernized' version of labourism for the 1990s and early twenty-first century. This point will be taken up again in the concluding chapter.

Conclusion – the continuity of labourism

This all too brief overview of a history of the British Labour Party in the twentieth century has been undertaken with a view to establishing the continuity and consistency of ideology, policy and practice right throughout this period and to characterize this as 'labourism'. It has concentrated upon the party's stated aims and objectives throughout the last 101 years. This will undoubtedly be seen by some as too simplistic and to be 'over-homogenizing' the actual history, which, without doubt, has been a period of a great many economic, social and political convulsions within Britain's borders and beyond. But this book does not argue that the Labour Party has not changed at all, either in its modus operandi or particularly as regards relative right and left-wing influence, throughout its history. Clearly the latter occurred during the late 1970s and early 1980s, the most recent period when the left were in the ascendancy. However, it is the main contention of this book that the theory and practice of the British Labour Party has not changed fundamentally since the party's inception. Thus the swings from right to left and back again have easily been accommodated within the boundaries of labourism.

Chapter 3

Sheffield – a case study of labourism

Introduction

This chapter is an empirical case study of the Sheffield labour movement from 1973 to 1998. It seeks to establish the responses of that labour movement to the decline of steel production and engineering as the predominant sources of employment in the city. It also looks at its involvement in the economic regeneration activities that have been and are currently taking place there. As such, it examines the roles of the trade unions, the Labour Party and, to a much lesser extent, the Communist Party. All of the latter have been involved in various institutions and organisations within the city and beyond, the most important of which are the Trades and Labour Council, the City Council, South Yorkshire County Council, the District Labour Party and the Trades Council. All of these feature extensively in the events of the twenty-five years covered in this chapter.

Perhaps one of the most important questions to answer is: 'why a case study of labour in Sheffield?' This question divides neatly into two parts: 'what is the purpose of the case study?' and 'why Sheffield?' The basic purpose of the study is to attempt to illustrate something of the general operation and processes of what has been characterized in this book as labourism. By examining the responses of a local labour movement to the decline of a major industry, as a source of employment, over a protracted time period, it is my intention to show something of how labourism operates generally and to provide specific examples of the characteristics outlined in Chapter One.

The choice of Sheffield as the subject for the study is anything but accidental. The personal reasons have been explained in the introduction. Sheffield, with its population of over half a million, is the fourth largest city in England. It is also, indisputably, a city built upon the cutlery, steel-producing and engineering industries. It was a centre for specialist steel production and engineering. Thus it can be said to be, at least in one sense, representative of large industrial, urban areas of Britain, the traditional 'heartlands' of Labour, and therefore of labourism. The strength and density of its labour movement, historically, will be examined later in the chapter. However, it is worthy of mention here that during the first half of the period under examination, and earlier, Sheffield had one of the strongest local labour movements in the country, if not in Western Europe. Sheffield does, therefore, present an example of a city and a local labour movement that are of considerable interest in their own right, and in many senses representative of Labour's heartlands.

Methodology

The main method used for the case study was that of semi-structured interviews of a small, but representative, sample of key participants in the local labour movement over the period being examined. Between the beginning of April and the end of July 1998, sixteen people were interviewed. They ranged from trade union shop stewards, convenors and branch secretaries, through city and county councillors, to council leaders and MPs.[129] Many of the people interviewed had held a number of labour movement positions during the period being examined, some in both the unions and the city council. Attempts were made to maintain a gender, ethnic and political (primarily left/right) balance. Attempts were also made to obtain interviews with three individuals who were considered to be key participants. The first was the Secretary of Sheffield Trades Council who, despite numerous and persistent approaches, did not respond. The second was the leader of the City Council, Mike Bower, who lost his seat in the local elections of May 1998. An interview that had been arranged before the election did not take place and there was no response to a subsequent approach. The third was a senior member of staff of Sheffield City Council who had been instrumental in its Employment Department and in developing the Cultural Industries Quarter. Numerous approaches received no reply.

As regards the method of semi-structured interviews, various 'field work' approaches were drawn upon in a very eclectic manner. These included the work of William Foote Whyte (1984), grounded theory, ethnomethodology and an oral history approach. However, the interviewing process drew only very loosely upon the first three of these approaches. While ethnomethodology claims that theory must be generated from the empirical, and grounded theory also highly values this approach, the method adopted here is based upon a completely different perspective. Instead of proceeding *from* the empirical to the theoretical, it uses the interviews to *test out* a hypothesis. This hypothesis, stating it simply, is that it is possible to characterize the ideas and actions of the British labour movement, both unions and party, over the last 101 years as 'labourism'. Furthermore, that this characterization accounts for and explains the motivations and policies of that movement over that time period.

The main aspect of the methodological approach taken was to have a common set of themes for each interview, to invite interviewees to speak on each of these subjects and to ensure that, in each interview, all of these themes were covered. Thus, all of the interviewees would be asked for their thoughts on, for example, the main reasons for the decline of steel and engineering as sources of employment in the city. It was emphasized that the interest was in the thoughts and feelings of the interviewee on all of the subjects rather than in facts and figures. They were interrupted only to clarify or expand upon a point. Some interviewees would talk at length on a particular subject and others would give very brief replies. No attempt was made to curtail any of the points being made unless they appeared to be completely irrelevant to the research topic. The interviews lasted between forty-five minutes and two hours, depending upon how much the interviewee had to say. Most of them lasted for approximately one hour.

Interviewing was chosen in preference to consulting primary or secondary literature because of the nature of the subject. Almost by definition, different participants in this type of case study are likely to have different conceptions of the nature of the problems, the solutions proffered, the actions taken and the results. While primary and secondary literature can sometimes reflect this variety, in this instance it seemed very important to go directly to the people who had themselves been intimately involved with, and affected by, the processes being studied. It did prove to be the case that a wide range of opinions were expressed on all of the issues mentioned above. It was also the case that there was simply insufficient primary and secondary literature available to carry out the task. All the material that was available was consulted.

However, there is another, and perhaps more important, reason for adopting the interview approach. Politics directly, and indirectly, affects people's lives. Their feelings and thoughts on any subject are influenced by their level of involvement. It thus seemed very appropriate to ask people directly involved in the process being studied what they felt and thought about these issues, both as labour movement activists and as employees and users of council services. Questions, therefore, were not restricted to their roles as trade unionists, councillors, politicians and campaigners. They also included subjects such as how they felt about being made redundant, what they felt about local swimming baths being closed down, and their thoughts about such things as the South Yorkshire Supertram. They were treated as both 'actors' in the process and 'recipients' of the results of that process.

Another important issue is that, despite appearances, Sheffield is not an island and the local-national link is emphasized by many interviewees. While the interviews tended to concentrate on local themes, clearly national events, particularly the effects of the Thatcher government, had a massive impact on the local economy and local politics. The case study is an attempt to illustrate a national argument by using local examples. The tension between the two is evident throughout the first half of the chapter. However, the second half will make an explicit case for the national relevance of most of the local examples covered.

In addition to the interviews, a number of primary and secondary literary sources were consulted, for two main reasons. First, simply to check or establish facts and figures such as dates, names of posts held, etc. Second, to provide a context within which some of the points being made in the interview could be understood and evaluated. A good example is the 'bottom-up' anti-paternalist approach to all of their work adopted in the early 1980s by Sheffield City Council, under the leadership of David Blunkett. This approach is explained in a pamphlet *Building from the Bottom, The Sheffield Experience* by David Blunkett and Geoff Green (1983) and provides a context within which to view and evaluate this strategy. However, as already mentioned, the literature on the general subject under investigation was scant.

Another very important point in favour of the interviewing method is that history can often be made to appear, in literature, as black and white when in fact it is often varying shades of grey. To take the example above, the literature generally portrays the early 1980s as a period when the 'Young Turks' on the City Council – Blunkett, Clive Betts and a number of others – were implementing this radical strategy of 'anti-paternalism' and empowerment of local people. However, when interviewees were asked about this, only a very small number enthusiastically embraced it and one, Mandy Siberry, who had been a NALGO shop steward at the council during that period, said '…in the early 80s , the council was incredibly paternalistic … David Blunkett was *incredibly* paternalistic as well – "It'll be all right with me, I know what we're doing"…' Most of the interviewees either ignored the question or played down its significance.

The purpose of the chapter, then, is to attempt to illustrate something of the *modus operandi* of labourism; what might be, and has been, in earlier chapters, termed 'the logic of labourism'. At first sight it might appear somewhat surprising that the interviewees held such widely divergent views. It might be expected, given that they are all members of the Sheffield labour movement, that they would speak with something resembling a single voice. However, the case has already been made that labourism represents something of a 'broad church' as regards ideologies, beliefs and values. Given that this is the case, it would be surprising *not* to find such divergent views. But it should be emphasized here that all the views represented in the case study can be situated, firmly and unequivocally, within the boundaries of labourism.

Why 1973-1998?

The choice of 1973 as the starting point of the period under study was not made arbitrarily. The global economic crisis caused in that year by the huge increase in the oil price charged by the OPEC countries had an undoubted effect on the steel-producing and engineering industries of Sheffield. It also appeared to me that the decline of these industries actually started at about that time. When one approaches such subjects, it is almost impossible to discover precisely when such things began. Indeed, there was a variety of responses from interviewees on this subject. Clive Betts, currently MP for Sheffield Attercliffe, and leader of Sheffield City Council from 1987 to 1992, dated the decline from the late 1960s. Ted Thorne, an Iron and Steel Trades Confederation (ISTC) Branch Secretary dates the appearance of short-time working back to the mid-

1950s. In fact, Ted's observations are confirmed by a report produced by the Sheffield Trades Council in 1982 which also dates the decline in employment in manufacturing back to the 1950s.[130] However, there was generally something of a consensus that the large numbers of redundancies and factory closures in these industries occurred between the mid-1970s and mid-1980s. It seemed appropriate, then, to look at the period 1973-1998, especially as the study of a quarter of a century provides the possibility of a calm and reflective, but certainly not completely detached, approach to the subject. This proved to be very much the case, with the interviewees being able to reflect upon matters and yet at the same time still have a high level of emotional and intellectual engagement.

One further thing should be mentioned here that may, at first sight, appear to be a major omission. There is no reference in this study to the cutlery industry. Sheffield's cutlery, in the post-war period, gained worldwide fame and was known for its high quality. The term *Made in Sheffield*, stamped on cutlery, became a byword for excellence. However, by the 1970s, the industry had already experienced serious decline and had ceased to be one of the major employers of labour in Sheffield. There were, and are still, some specialist manufacturers located there, but the mass volume cutlery industry shifted to the Far East during the 1960s.

Frequent mention will be made of Sheffield City Council. Within the text, and invariably within the interview comments quoted, the term 'the council' will refer to the City Council. South Yorkshire County Council was only in existence from 1973 to 1986, and is therefore not referred to with the same familiarity. Also, Sheffield has a very strong local dialect. When it was spoken, quotes from interviewees have been written in this dialect, given its strength and the nature of its use. There was some use of local colloquialisms, so it seemed entirely proper to transcribe these directly, rather than attempt to translate them into 'correct' English. Another point is that, because of interviewees' conversational style, which it seemed appropriate to preserve here, many of the quotations are of some length.

The strength of the Sheffield labour movement

I will begin by examining the nature and the sources of strength of the Sheffield labour movement. As with the other subjects, there is no absolute consensus about this. Dan Sequerra, a full-time official with the

Association of Scientific, Technical and Managerial Staffs (ASTMS) from 1975-1985 and Director of the Employment Department of the council from 1985-1990, made a very compelling argument that any investigation into labourism in Sheffield must start with Jack Murphy and the Shop Stewards' movement in Sheffield and Clydeside in the 1920s. Roger Barton, Sheffield's MEP and Sheffield City Councillor for eighteen years before that, insisted that the strength of the local movement started in the 1950s and possibly earlier.

It is the case that the city council has had an almost unbroken record of Labour control since 1926. In 1932 and from 1968 to 1969 the Conservatives took control for one year only. Apart from these very brief interludes, Labour had (until 1999) ruled continuously. This Labour authority had been, in turn, a provider of clean water and sanitation, regulated abattoirs, a clearer of 'slum' housing and provider of new, low-rent, municipally-owned housing and many more things. It was generally perceived as both pro-active and efficient. The term 'the corporation', which was used and still is by some people in Sheffield, is generally an affectionate label. Sheffield has consistently returned Labour MPs in five of the six parliamentary constituencies since the Second World War, usually with very large majorities. Taylor et al (1996) note: 'In Sheffield (Brightside), covering the industrial East End, the Labour vote, in local parlance, was not so much counted as "weighed".'[131] This electoral strength is unquestionable. In 1973, at the beginning of the period under examination, Labour held sixty-nine out of the ninety seats on the council. The electoral strength of the Labour Party in Sheffield, after the Second World War, is very well known.

From an electoral or political perspective, therefore, there is no doubt that Sheffield was (and perhaps still is) a 'Labour City'. However, it is very important to try and discover the roots of this electoral success for Labour, and there is no doubt they are to be found in the powerful trade unionism of the manufacturing industries of the city.

The high degree of unionization of manufacturing and the high levels of membership within factories in Sheffield is very well known. The vast majority of factories were unionized and in each factory membership was virtually 100%. In 1975, the Amalgamated Engineering Union (AEU), as it then was, had 30,000 members in Sheffield. The unions with the largest membership were the AEU, the ISTC and the Transport and General Workers' Union (TGWU). Smaller unions, but nevertheless with some political influence within Sheffield, were the Electrical, Electronic, Telecommunications and Plumbing Union (EETPU) and the National Union of Sheet Metal Workers, Coppersmiths, Heating and Domestic Engineers.

It is perhaps worth emphasizing that steel production and engineering were overwhelmingly the main manufacturing industries in the city until the 1980s. *Bulk* steel production was predominant in neighbouring Rotherham, while Sheffield tended to concentrate on special steels of various kinds, particularly alloys including stainless steel.

Discussing the relationship between the trade unions and political activity, Roger Barton, referring to a period starting in the 1950s, stated: '...what there was very much a participatory exercise on was local government matters and the fact that that you'd got vibrant manufacturing industry and a high degree of unionization meant that you'd got people who'd had that background of activity, whose minds were exercised to wider questions than just industrial working conditions, wages and such-like, and who were concerned about living conditions generally outside the workplace. With rents, with availability of housing, with decent health conditions, water supplies and so on...This is the point – your bedrock was the activity in the industrial workplace and that threw up some people – maybe 10% of the people who were very active at plant and then district level on trade union matters – they were then creamed off or sucked off into wider political questions and you'd got the...Trades and Labour Council...it achieved a two-way interactivity, so the councillors were of that background and often continued to work in those situations and so there was a natural two way flow.' Barton makes it quite clear, elsewhere in the interview, that this situation prevailed until the 1970s and perhaps even into the 1980s.

This quote summarizes relatively concisely what most of the interviewees had to say about the unity of the industrial and political sections of the Sheffield labour movement. It also draws attention to the central role of the Trades and Labour Council. Dan Sequerra states that '...up until the '50s, I think, ...the traditions in towns like Sheffield was for a joint Trades and Labour Council. Because they needed to separate, politically, the Labour Party from the more variegated trade unions, a lot of trades and labour councils were split. The right wing of the Labour Party didn't find it very comfortable to be in situations where the District Labour Party was subject in any way to influence. Now, the Trades and

Labour Council in Sheffield stood out against the general line and it was the last trades and labour council to be split. It wasn't split I think till the late '60s, early 70s…' This unity cannot be overemphasized. Through initially the Trades and Labour Council and, after the split, the District Labour Party and the Trades Council, there was tremendous solidarity between trade unionists and local politicians; in fact they were often the same people. In turn, they made almost the entire policy of the Labour Group on Sheffield City Council. The Trades and Labour Council was a joint body of representatives of trade unions and the Labour Party. The Labour Party nationally decided in the early 1970s to divide the two and so Sheffield, reluctantly, had to abide by this ruling. They were divided into the Trades Council and the District Labour Party. However, as a number of interviewees mentioned, they continued to work as if they were one body for many years after this. Below, Dan refers to the joint executive of the two bodies. It was the case that right up until the early 1990s the District Labour Party continued to have tremendous influence on the policies and actions of the Labour Group on the council.

The importance of these bodies within the community generally should also be emphasized. Alan Wigfield, who was Chair of Housing and Chief Whip on the council, said that '…the Trades Council was regarded of being such importance that the local newspaper, *The Star*, used to send their journalists along to report on events at the meeting and they'd get a decent write-up the following night. All I can say [is] that the journalists they sent along was always an NUJ member and he or she was obviously sympathetic to the trade union movement. When you get a full report of what occurred, including mug-shots and so-and-so said this…it was regarded as being an important and influential body.' Every interviewee who made reference to the Trades and Labour Council, the Trades Council and the District Labour Party emphasized their centrality as regards decision-making and policy formulation within the Sheffield labour movement. This function of these bodies, uniting the industrial and political sections of the movement, is essential to this examination of the local movement.

Dan made the above comment about the Trades and Labour Council in the context of the influence of the Communist Party in the Sheffield movement. This influence, which was strongest in the AEU but was present in other unions as well, could potentially have been very divisive. However, all of the interviewees who make comments on it stress the co-operation between the two parties. Dan Sequerra again: 'They worked through various organisations – the Trades and Labour Council – the Trades Council had a very strong CP influence – so that was one, and the joint executive of the Trades Council and the District Labour Party was a mechanism for aligning policies.' It is quite difficult to gauge the extent of the influence of the Communist Party in Sheffield labour movement, because generally, and perhaps not surprisingly, interviewees were reluctant to talk about it. However, out of the sixteen interviewees, three had been very active members of the Communist Party. The most famous Sheffield Communist of all, George Caborn, the trade union Convenor of English Steel Corporation (and the father of Richard Caborn, the current MP for Sheffield, Central and the Minister for the Environment, Transport and the Regions) was awarded the freedom of the city in 1982, just before he died. It appears that the Communist Party was very strong in the AEU. Peter Birch, an ex-Communist himself, confirmed this and Terry Gardner commented: 'Oh, ah you'd got to be in ' Communist Party to be on ' executive in Sheffield 28th Confed., or so they say.' The 28th Confederation was an engineering confederation.

The influence of Communism specifically within the AEU, overwhelmingly the main engineering union in Sheffield, provoked the possibility of another cleavage within the movement. The Iron and Steel Trades Confederation, which was the main trade union in the steel works, would not have been at all sympathetic to the Communist Party. Yet a very small number of its local representatives were Communists and the rest were generally happy to work with the Communists in the AEU when necessary. It appears that divisions would have arisen at more senior levels within the two unions. Another potential source of division is that between engineers as craftsmen and steelworkers as skilled, semi-skilled and unskilled workers. That is, between the workforces of the two main industries. The division is clearly there. However, from the interviews it appears that it was a source of little contention. This issue will be returned to later in the chapter.

One final point to be made on the strength of the labour movement relates to what might be called 'the Sheffield factor'. The city, surrounded by seven hills, is geographically somewhat isolated, and is, even today, relatively culturally homogenous for such a large city. Sheffielders often refer to it as the 'biggest village in England' and there is an intimacy and familiarity amongst its population that many visitors find surprising and pleasant. This can be, and often was, linked to the near hegemony of Labour in the city. Barton, again: '…this natural friendliness thing that is around in Sheffield on top of that – when I was District Secretary the theme that I used to tap up most was 'Are you proud of Sheffield? – of course you are, vote Labour.' I tried to make the connection, automatic connection between the two.'

This pride in Sheffield is a very strong and sometimes intangible factor in people's lives. It is also something that might account for the pride that steel workers and engineers, historically, took in their products. At first sight this may appear somewhat contradictory. Sheffield was a place where trade unionism was very powerful and one might expect that this would generate a sense of 'separateness' from the employer and therefore a process of distancing oneself from the product. Nothing could be further from the truth. Peter Birch, an engineer and trade union Convenor at a company called Cravens stated: '…we were proud of the product which was absolutely first-class machinery made by a workforce that was 90% fully-skilled and 10% unskilled and semi-skilled – and we took a pride in what we produced -…' Dan Sequerra is more eloquent: 'For example forging, now there was not a more skilled person amongst the skilled working-class than a head forgeman at Firth Brown's. Because he had a piece of steel….and his skill was in by looking at the colour of the metal, the temperature, the right time to get the forges working to press down the shape, yes. This was, its intuitive skill which is there, but these were the *real* skilled men and around them they had an aura. And of course the trade union organisation was built around these type of things… These were people – this is the cream of the working class here in terms of skill and understanding and knowledge in its form that is absorbed through every pore of your body, and you're looking for the slightest change in colour, temperature – and they would give instructions to the others.'

In turn this pride in 'the job' produced a highly disciplined workforce. Both the trade unions and the Communist Party can take some credit for this discipline. Ted Thorne, an ISTC Branch Secretary, on the trade unions and organisation of the plant, said: 'Yes, they played a part in it… they, to an extent, …disciplined the members, in so far as there were rules, regulations…' Dan Sequerra said: '…the trade union perspective on it – I don't want to romanticize it – but…some of the pride in

Sheffield was about the pride in the nature of the working process and the organisation of labour. Despite battling hard for the conditions, they still produced good product…so, I think…this pride is double-edged in a way. I don't think it produced divided loyalties, it enhanced and encouraged the trade union organisation.' The Communist Party, primarily through the AEU in Sheffield, contributed tremendously towards this industrial discipline. They equated trade union organisation, good wages and conditions, with good organisation of the work process and factory generally. Therefore, it appears that the trade unions and the Communist Party did not in any way attempt to wreck industrial organisation. Instead, they enhanced the efficiency of the company by disciplining the workforce and by contributing to a sense of pride in the job. All of the interviewees who referred to the unions and the Communist Party, made comments which supported this view. Additionally, most, if not all, of the interviewees who were trade unionists casually referred to the company they worked for as 'we' or 'us' on numerous occasions, suggesting loyalty to and identification with that company.

This situation was all very well during a period of economic boom, and Sheffield's steel and engineering industries certainly experienced boom during the 1950s and 1960s. However, the economic landscape changed rapidly and dramatically in the second half of the 1970s and first half of the 1980s and it is the response of this strong and proud trade union movement to these massive changes that is of particular interest here.

To summarize this section, Sheffield's labour movement, from the 1950s right through to the first half of the 1980s, was very strong indeed. This strength was based upon the high degree of unionization in the steel-producing and engineering industries, the unity of the industrial and political elements of the movement, the 'free movement' between the two, the development of democratic institutions such as the Trades and Labour Council, and later the joint executive of the Trades Council and the District Labour Party, and, it has been argued, the relative cultural homogeneity of the local population and local pride in place and product. The relatively strong influence of the Communist Party and the historical divisions between the 'craft' unions, particularly the AEU, and others failed to diminish this strength. In fact, the former enhanced it. The labour movement of Sheffield was one of the strongest in the country and beyond. However, in the early 1970s the strength of Sheffield's traditional industries began to be challenged and it is the response of this powerful labour movement to those developments that is the subject of the next section.

Explanations for the decline of steel and engineering

Whether the beginnings of the decline of steel and engineering date back to the early 1970s, the late 1960s or even the mid-1950s, by the late 1970s it was obvious that something was going terribly wrong. Between 1971 and 1976 over 9,000 jobs in steel were lost in Sheffield and Rotherham. This represented a 16% reduction. Between 1978 and 1981, approximately 18,700 jobs were lost. In 1981 alone, 12,000 people were made redundant. By October of that year, 38,000 people were unemployed in Sheffield, the highest figure since 1934.[132] Large factories that were household names in Sheffield, such as Hadfields, Osborn and Firth Brown, were either closing or making huge redundancies. Industries that people had taken for granted for many years appeared to be 'going under', and people in the local labour movement, along with other economic commentators, tried to find the reason. This study does not have access to the answers that were proposed at the time, but it is able to investigate the question with the hindsight of approximately twenty years. The wide variety of answers given by the interviewees to the question: 'what do you think were the main causes of the decline of Sheffield's manufacturing industries?' is fascinating: from 'Maggie Thatcher' through to 'a lack of investment in plant and equipment'.

Roger Barton referred to the decline as 'de-industrialization'. Alan Jones, a councillor on South Yorkshire County Council from 1981 to 1986 said: 'All the time we'd been producing top quality steel, acknowledged as such throughout the world, and the concern was they were being undercut by the common market countries, seeing imports of cheap, subsidized steel from abroad, from Italy and all over the place, when our steel wasn't or didn't seem to be subsidized. It was as though the government at a European level was letting this happen...The other thing that led to the demise of the steel industry was the fact that on the bulk steel producing side, the Common Market was giving massive subsidies to pay for redundancies, in order to control the steel-making capacity in the EEC. People were being bought off, to some extent, with *quite good* redundancy packages.'

Clive Betts, MP for Sheffield, Attercliffe and leader of Sheffield City Council from 1987 to 1992, said: 'I remember working as a teenager, before I went to University, at English Steel, and plant and equipment in the late 1960s that had been imported from Germany at the end of the First World War, second-hand and it was still going...we weren't competing for the mass orders, were picking up the bits and pieces in some sections of the industry. On the other hand, the early 1980s had an added problem that some firms had begun to invest and begun to recognise the problems of lack of long-term investment, just at the time that the new Tory government under Thatcher put the squeeze on – interest rates went up, there was a clamping-down on domestic demand, and those firms had invested and taken out quite high levels of borrowing and got absolutely screwed through the floor for the investment they had carried out. Demand fell and the cost of the borrowings went up...'

Bill Michie, MP for Sheffield, Heeley and long-time Treasurer of the Labour Party Campaign Group, suggested: 'The big problem came when there was an agreement in Europe to massively cut down on steel production, of which, I still maintain to this day, the UK took more than their fair share of cuts...I would have preferred each nation to have made its own decision in the sense that we could have rationalized things better. I mean, the whole thing moved too fast. We had the problem then of MacGregor coming in basically to kill most of the industry, as he did with the mineworkers as well.'

David Blunkett, who was the leader of Sheffield City Council from 1980 to 1987, had the following to say: '...the first realization that there was something very severely amiss was when the Tories decided to take the steel workers on in 1980. The steelworkers were not militant, the ISTC were not looking for a fight. The decision basically to refuse them a pay increase was a deliberate act of provocation and it did become clear very quickly that's what it was. And they were looking, spoiling for a fight in order to link taking on the unions in terms of changing the pattern, together with their decision to capitulate in terms of the European quotas...It all related to Britain enthusiastically embracing the Single Market before it was actually written into the European law, and wanting the removal of European subsidies. Steel and related production and enthusiastically going along with the Commission's desire to provide quite draconian reductions in steel production. The problem was that

Britain did it and others didn't. There's still hidden subsidies now in Germany and Austria and Spain, whilst we've eliminated ours. They did through – not just direct subsidy – but the subsidy of electricity, gas production. So they were providing cheap electricity to arc furnaces and still are in Germany and Spain.'

Dan Sequerra was much more dramatic: '…'79 came – that was the rudest shock that the system just couldn't live with. I mean – I couldn't believe what was happening – factories just shut in a matter of twelve to twenty-four months, big, big factories just closed…because of their [the Tory government's] industrial policy, ye – they went with the market. Sheffield had been cushioned from the market..'

Pat Heath, who was Chair of Social Services on Sheffield City Council from 1986 to 1991 was very eloquent on the subject: 'The late '70s from Thatcher getting in and perhaps even a little bit before that, when the old Labour government was adopting monetarist tactics…as a way of managing the economy – when Thatcher got in – that really set the seal on it – steel strike, factory closures, mass redundancies in Sheffield – statements coming out and a determination in government, clearly explicit, that organized collective of trade unions, manufacturing – all was going to be subject to monetary forces…A combination of features I guess. Partly, political determination to pursue monetary forces and economic theory at any cost – irrespective of the damage that it did to communities. Determination politically to crush any political opposition through trade unions or local government, combined with world-wide global features – rising oil prices, squeezing of demand, monetary 'compaction'…of the economy…all of which has a knock-on for steel and other related products. So I guess a combination of those features screwed the life out of the employers who tried to screw the life out of the workforce.'

Ted Thorne was much more succinct: 'Technology, its as simple as that …Progress. Inevitable.' Terry Gardner, another Branch Secretary in the ISTC, said something very similar: '…its technology, cus you can't get round the end figure that there's more [steel] produced than there ever were. It with thousands of people less… during First World War, or round about that period, Hadfield's employed 40,000… there's 40,000 in all our union across country now… its technology really.' This last point, that there is currently more steel being produced in Sheffield than ever before, with a dramatically reduced workforce, will be returned to later in the chapter.

The steel industry was nationalized, for the second time, in 1967. Fourteen companies became the new British Steel Corporation (BSC). This left a large number of companies in private ownership. It was de-nationalized by Mrs. Thatcher's government in 1988, but parts of BSC had already been sold off to the private sector during the 1980s. Nationalization and de-nationalization had a huge impact on the industry as a whole, but there is insufficient space here to examine it properly. The two interviewees that represented the ISTC had a great deal to say about the period of nationalization. Ted Thorne said, again very succinctly, 'To sum it up,… it would have been far better if they'd sent the population, in turn, on holiday in the Bahamas, than spend all the money that they spent. A lot of it was wasted. Grandiose plans, the empire-building and that went on considerably…that all…started altering… in the '70s when they started closing…and demanning plants, and its still ongoing…as a consequence of being denationalized…quite frankly, what I observed of the period of nationalization, I would never, and I used to be a great advocate of nationalization in my time,…advocate a similar experience.' He went on: 'Well, it mainly became a job for the boys. There were that many management structures, it was wasteful and inefficient… the whole object of nationalization was to serve the public. It dint work that way. But now… how many members did they 'ave, the ISTC? Something like – well above 100,000. I don't think they've got 20,000 now. … The manpower that was involved at that time. The manpower involved now, which has been as a consequence of the denationalization process. Far more efficient and it produces more steel.' His colleague, Terry Gardner, was equally critical: '…there were a lot o' silly money spent in British Steel. I'll say that as a Labour Party member – somebody who at that time believed in nationalization, not necessarily now – not for ' steel industry. For other things I still do…people were allowed to build empires…but underlying this, if there'd been no investment from the government. there'd been no steel industry …it just wunt 'ave been there…gone. Because it was technically backward apart from a few exceptions…' Bill Michie, who worked and was a shop steward in the steel industry before and during nationalization, was only slightly less scathing: 'There's been a lot of disappointments at the way nationalization turned out, in terms of job security and massive changes. Some were inevitable anyway by the change in markets and changing world, but …even in a nationalized industry there were massive mistakes made – re-organization for re-organization's sake…it tended to be run by a bunch of bureaucrats rather than people that fully understood the management side, not all of them, some were very good of course.'

There was, then, a consensus that nationalization in the steel industry was nearly disastrous. Importantly, the huge processes of nationalization and then de-nationalization have had massive detrimental effects on the industry, particularly its capacity to be internationally competitive. It is perhaps worth noting that all the interviewees were critical of the form that nationalization of the steel industry had taken, rather than the principle of nationalization, which, in fact, they favoured.

The most novel reason given for the rapid decline of Sheffield's industries was provided by Dan Sequerra: '…the Tories had it in for Sheffield, ever since we all stood outside the Cutlers Hall and gave Mrs. Thatcher an unwelcoming, and she never forgave us for that, in 1983. She was bitter about that. That's why the World Student Games never got any money. There was no other reason… She was horrified – she saw all this screaming mob outside …the Cutler's Feast…Roger Barton and I…we were organizing this stuff through the District Labour Party and the Trades Council…she never forgave Sheffield…oh, ye it was known amongst the …government officials.' Dan is referring here to a very large and noisy demonstration by the local movement outside the Cutler's Hall when Mrs. Thatcher was the Guest of Honour at the Cutler's Feast.

It can be seen, therefore, that a wide range of reasons were given for the decline of steel and engineering in Sheffield. These can be summarized as: under-investment in plant and equipment for many years prior to the period under examination; the increase in oil prices in 1973; the election of Mrs. Thatcher's government in 1979 and its pursuit of monetarist economic policies; the removal of subsidies from the European Community and Thatcher's enthusiastic support for this; the introduction of new technology that massively reduced labour-intensity in production; nationalization/de-nationalization and finally the idea that Thatcher 'had it in for Sheffield'. All of them, with the possible exception of the, perhaps, fanciful idea of Thatcher's personal retaliation, contributed towards the downfall of Sheffield's staple industries. There is no doubt that by the 1970s, as a result of under-investment in plant and equipment, Sheffield companies were unable to compete with some of their international competitors. This was compounded by the huge increase in oil prices and the removal of European subsidies, and was compounded still further by governmental economic and political activity during the 1980s. One of the explicit intentions of the monetarist economic policies of the Conservative government was to massively reduce the power of the trade unions. It was inevitable, then, that Sheffield, with its powerful labour movement would be affected. This inevitability is based upon the government's absolute determination to pursue this policy without regard, as Pat Heath stated, for any of its social consequences. It is important to emphasize the multiplicity of factors rather than a single reason or small number of reasons.

These are the explanations for the decline which can be fairly clearly identified approximately twenty years later. However, they were not at all clear between 1975 and 1985 and the effects on the people of Sheffield were devastating. Pat Heath said: 'Oh yes, flattened communities, flattened individuals, flattened the economy locally. The tragic thing is that so much human experience went on the scrap heap…' Pat's few words sum up and yet mask a great deal of human misery. Large numbers of people, mainly men, who had earned higher than average rates of pay, had the dignity and pride of working within an efficient productive industry and, in some cases, had the status of skill and/or labour movement position, were made redundant in a very short period of time, with very little prospect of any alternative employment in the foreseeable future. The concomitant social effects of this have been well documented in books by Beattie (1986) and Taylor et al (1996) and will not be repeated here. However, it should be briefly noted that huge increases in crime, domestic conflict, drug and alcohol abuse all became a feature of life in Sheffield's poorer areas during the 1980s and 1990s, as they did in many other parts of the country. Perhaps one of the differences in Sheffield was that these things were particularly noticeable in a population that had previously experienced high levels of employment, a huge pride in work and product and a highly developed work ethic.

Before discussing the responses of the labour movement to the decline of these industries it should be noted that the decline in steel production was essentially one in *employment* rather than *output*. Virtually every interviewee, and certainly all of the senior politicians, made the comment that 'there is more steel being produced in Sheffield now than there ever was'! It is the case that a very large quantity of steel is currently being produced in Sheffield with approximately one-tenth of the previous workforce. This issue will be examined in detail later in the chapter and will be merely noted here as an important point in relation to steel production. However, the same cannot be said of engineering. Engineering companies that used to employ very large numbers of people have disappeared and have not been replaced by more efficient, capital-intensive ones.

The responses of the local movement to decline: the unions

Peter Birch said: 'The actual struggles and battles for the right to work and the opposition against job losses never really took off...Certainly by '84, things were extremely difficult...but there was never a major fight-back against massive job losses...' Instead, traditional practices such as 'short-time working' were pursued. Peter Birch explained: '...historically we'd always had a good track record of sharing short-term problems, in engineering and in steel, whereby we frequently had periods of short-time working and it was a feature of that period – '75 up to '84... we obviously used to argue in principle, managements at that time used to say 'we've got to make twenty people redundant out of x number of hundred and we used to equate that and say 'no, we're not having *anybody* made redundant – that twenty people equates to x number of hours that you wish to lose out of a wages system and production, and we used to spread it – it was a fairly common feature to have short periods of short time working – usually weekends off, laid off after Thursday night and start work the following Tuesday.' In 1981, 16,000 people were on short-time working.[133]

Other interviewees also acknowledged the lack of an adequate general response to the decline. However, the national steel strike of 1980 was an example of a major fightback on the part of the steel unions. On the December 30th 1979 the ISTC called a national steel strike in response to a derisory pay offer, with conditions attached, from the British Steel Corporation (BSC). This initially included only workers at BSC plants but it was extended at the end of January to private sector workers. This was a momentous strike for the ISTC, their first national one since 1926, and was widely perceived as a confrontation with the recently elected Conservative government. There was a call, not officially endorsed, for a 20% pay increase with 'no strings attached', from the South Yorkshire steelworkers. The trade unions officially on strike in

1980 were the ISTC, the National Union of Blastfurnacemen (NUB), the TGWU, the General and Municipal Workers Union (GMWU) and the constituent members of the National Craftsmen's Co-ordinating Committee (NCCC), which included the AEU. However, this included only members in steel-producing companies, not those in engineering. The National Union of Railwaymen (NUR) and the Associated Society of Locomotive Engineers and Firemen (ASLEF) supported the strike by blocking the movement of steel by rail.

In Sheffield, ISTC members enthusiastically supported the strike and mass pickets were seen at a number of large private steel companies. Some sections of the AEU in engineering companies unofficially supported the strike by boycotting steel produced locally. There were head-on confrontations with the police, the most famous of which resulted in the closure of a very large steel company, Hadfields, on February 14th. The strike, symbolically and actually, galvanized support from the local labour movement in much the same way as the miner's strike would nationally a few years later. It became a focus of early resistance to Thatcher's government. Dan Sequerra gives his version of the events: '…in the steel strike they battled here something enormous, I mean I had members (in ASTMS) who refused to cross picket lines 'cos we weren't officially involved in the steel strike at national level but I had about 500 members refusing to cross picket lines, de facto on strike. We had meetings in the City Hall, we had mass pickets, in fact it was over one of the factories in Sheffield that the High Court injunction was, and there was a time, the only time Thatcher was vulnerable, in my opinion, was in the middle of the steel strike when a High Court judge, when the courts ruled against the employers and gave rights to picketing, but…the problem was that the TUC at national level weakened in the face because Thatcher called their bluff. She was vulnerable – …about a week or two's period when Thatcher could have gone.'

On the April 1st 1980, the strike was called off. Whether it was lost or 'drawn' depends upon one's perspective. David Blunkett, the current MP for Sheffield, Brightside and Secretary of State for Education and Employment, said: 'I took over as leader [of Sheffield City Council] in May 1980 and we were struggling immediately with the aftermath of the demoralization of the strike. They were defeated basically. It was a great morale blow and affected the psyche I think of people in the area.' Ted Thorne, who had been a member of the national negotiating team for the ISTC, said: 'Well it failed in this context – as a consequence of it, a lot o' jobs were shed. The negotiations weren't solely about pay, but as a consequence that's when the big 'ammer came down and started shedding labour. They say as in the same context as Scargill failed – 'cos they shut three parts of 'is industry down.' Terry Gardner, Ted's colleague in the ISTC has a slightly different perspective: 'At the end of it, when they did make a settlement, a lot o' people went ballistic and said we've been out three month, so we'd a' stopped another three. We thought [Bill] Sirs sold us out to be honest… I wunt say it was a total defeat. It weren't a victory either…a draw probably…us and Scotsmen were two militant areas…we thought we'd been selt out because we were prepared to 'ang out for a bigger basic settlement wi' no strings. The deal 'ad all sorts o' strings – shedding jobs… the old Sheffield division of British Steel, the job losses were round about 1200… when you look back, I wunt say it was a defeat but I certainly couldn't portray it as a glorious victory either.'

As for the reasons given for the end of the strike, Terry Gardner cited the 'sell-out' by the leadership. Pat Heath said: 'A number of issues I guess. There was a strong base of support in Sheffield – and certainly the trade unions concerned. But as time went on, people start to feel the pinch, and its very difficult for one group of workers in a particular area to sustain something like that indefinitely, if the employers are determined to sit it out. And the police increasingly and law and order forces, were determined to clamp down. I think at that point people start to, not drift back, but it becomes difficult to sustain it. As I say, unless you've been in that situation, its hard to imagine, going for much more than a few weeks without any source of income coming in – because you're not entitled to benefits and things like that…' Dan Sequerra offered the following: 'I think that the view from Sheffield was that the national leadership was poor – and they did all they could here. They overcame some very difficult problems in relation to the AEU, the CP was not totally convinced of the steel strike …cos they questioned the leadership of the ISTC that was primarily right-wing Labour.' This reminds us of Miliband's view that 'betrayal' of their membership by labour leaders is inherent in the 'logic of labourism'.

Additionally, there were a number of important individual strikes and other actions taken in response to the announcement of job losses, most notably at Snow's (a company specializing in grinding), Plansees, Davy Instruments, Jewel Razor (whose workforce were on strike for three months), Orgreave Pit and a very large company, Firth Brown's. However, in the end, all these heroic efforts achieved very little.

The major question to be answered is – why, given the strength of the Sheffield labour movement, when faced by the imminent decline and possible destruction of its major industries, did its trade unions do so little? Answers to this question vary. Peter Birch again: '...the timing of things in Sheffield, I might not be exactly perfect on dates and times,... when the Tory party under Margaret Thatcher in '79, when they started off on their programme in doing a whole range of things, for instance in 1981 – they removed the link between earnings and state pensions – and people could see the writing on the wall – when they turned their attention to the trade unions, certainly the dispute which they created against the miners did more than destroy the mining unions and shut the pits – it *also* put the frighteners on the rest of the trade union movement – and basically how it was timed in Sheffield ...during that twelve months dispute, we were finding it difficult to raise the moral and financial support although we did a lot for the miners, because we in steel and engineering, *at that same time*, it all happened together, basically the steel industry and engineering plants were going down like a pack o' cards in Sheffield during that twelve months of the miners dispute. People had said – if the miners, with their track record, can't stop job losses and pits closing, how can we stop the redundancies or this factory closing... Ye, I mean, its hard to put your finger on it afterwards, but ye we could see it coming, and basically the answers to it, everything got chucked in ' pot together. Perhaps if the steel and engineering job losses had come at a different time to the pit strike, if they'd been *separated* from them, we might have been able to 'ave built up better support and ensured that the miners won that one – certainly by the time we'd got to the miners, *a lot* of engineering jobs had gone in Sheffield and more were going – ye, on hindsight we could see it coming.'

Bill Michie suggested that the disunity of the unions in steel and engineering contributed: '...as unions we had a problem once we were nationalized because...they encouraged the staff to form their own association, which was called SIMA, Steel Industry Management Association, which obviously split the workforce...straight down the middle between so-called white-collar and blue-collar. The problem was ...there was, in a sense, a divide and rule. So you'd got the Iron and Steel Confederation, SIMA, AEU, or should we say the craft union, which didn't help as far as unity organisation was concerned, but we managed for so long but once the steel industry started going downhill, we were getting depleted one by one.' Interestingly, this contradicts the idea described earlier that the unions generally all worked well together in Sheffield.

Ted Thorne and Terry Gardner suggested that the introduction of new technology accounts for Sheffield's decline and, furthermore, that it was inevitable. Both acknowledged that, at the time, they fought this decline strongly and vociferously, yet Ted stated: 'What's life about? – its about moving on all the time. Life dunt stand still…For Christ's sake, the bloody Luddites never did any good.' This self-characterization of 'Luddite' or machine-breaker, and the notion of 'technological determinism', are very interesting and will be looked at later after the local labour movement's political responses to decline have been examined.

The council's initiatives

The response of the trade unions to the devastation of Sheffield's staple industries has been examined in some detail. What of the political or party response? To some extent the division is somewhat artificial given the unity of the industrial and political wings of the local movement. As we have seen, even as late as the 1980s the District Labour Party and the Trades Council had an enormous amount of influence on the policies and actions of the ruling Labour Group on Sheffield City Council. Sometimes the same people were involved in all three and, as before, the District Labour Party provided the guidance and context within which the Labour Group made its decisions.

But in fact the visible responses of the industrial and political sections of the local movement were quite different. While the trade unions appeared to be unprepared, powerless and left floundering for an appropriate response, the Labour Group on the council, under the new leadership of David Blunkett from May 1980, threw itself into a programme of action that was intended to counter the worst effects of the economic crisis. The most visible aspect of this was the creation of the Employment Department in 1981. This is one of Sheffield City Council's most celebrated (on the left of the movement) and controversial (mainly on the right) strategic actions during the period when Blunkett was leader and the council was vigorously pursuing its 'municipal socialism' approach. The Employment Department was set up to 'intervene' in the local economy, to assist, in whatever way it could: companies on the verge of bankruptcy; people wanting to set up a new enterprise; workers who wanted to run a company that was failing, as a co-operative; and provide general advice and assistance on such matters. Very importantly, it was also set up to undertake research on a long-term viable local economic strategy. Bill Michie, who was the first chair of the Employment Department, said: 'The argument was that if you've children, they need educating, that's the responsibility of the council. If you've got any problems as far as family life is concerned, you've got your social services, so if you've got a problem of losing your job, why can't the council provide a service for that as well, that was the logic behind it.' This, at first sight, seems a perfectly reasonable notion but it had never been tried before: Sheffield was the first local authority to set up such a department. However, many people, including central government and some Labour councillors in Sheffield, didn't agree. They didn't believe that employment was an appropriate area for a local authority to be involved in. Right from the start though, the 'Young Turks' (as Peter Horton, one-time Chair of Education and Lord Mayor referred to them) who had taken over the council in 1980 were ambitious and radical in their plans and actions. Large amounts of resources were channelled into the Employment Department. Bill Michie again: '...we had no expertise in the council as far as creating or protecting jobs was concerned, so we actually went out to the private sector, recruiting new officers, including accountants and treasurers and lawyers...and so we built up a fairly big department, people from universities to come and join us, redundant steel workers, engineers, shop stewards who had their own expertise...'

The budget allocated to the department was generous. Bill Michie claimed that they could spend £50,000 a month, if necessary, without going to a full council meeting for approval. Bill emphasized the financial assistance given to ailing companies, which mainly had the effect of prolonging their demise rather than making them successful. He also spoke of the setting up of small worker co-operatives. Blunkett said something slightly different: 'We were looking to try and provide an intermediate labour market before...the concept had been pulled together...We got the idea of research leading to production and marketing. We therefore made some progress, again offering an alternative, saying there was a third way.' According to Blunkett the third way was '…somewhere between the free market and Thatcher and an old Labourist – we must keep things as they are, we must just defend what we've got.' However, both he and Bill acknowledged that they were 'fire-fighting'. Blunkett used the 'King Canute' analogy, as did Ted Thorne when referring to trying to stop technological advance.

The Employment Department changed its remit somewhat when Bill Michie was elected to parliament in 1983 and was replaced as chair by Helen Jackson, the current MP for Sheffield, Hillsborough. It then became the Department for Employment and Economic Development (DEED). Helen described the difference: '…[it] included most of the strategic work on training, and on equal opportunities. So it was under our department, we sort of pioneered new training approaches both on technology, on access, access technology centre for unemployed people. On women's carpentry, women's joinery workshop we funded, women's plastering training project, Asian training project, lots of Afro-Caribbean enterprise centres, and a Pakistan Muslim centre – so we went into equal opportunities economic development and spent quite a lot of money. And, because this is the one that's really come to fruition in a way, we went quite heavily, again from the point of view that this was something for the future, into popular culture. I don't know if you've been there lately – the National Centre for Popular Music started right back in 1983/84.' She explains the reasons for the change of direction for the department: 'I was never very keen on the rescue package approach. I think it did get some bad publicity. You never knew whether it would be – you know – just throwing public money away.' In fact, the changes in 1983 were perhaps more substantial than Helen suggests.

Helen referred here to 'popular culture', and the Cultural Industries Quarter, where the National Centre for Popular Music is situated, is one of DEED's lasting initiatives. It started out in 1983 with the creation of Red Tape Studios, a suite of music recording studios, where local people could come and learn the techniques of recording. This was a big success. The Northern Media School got involved in the quarter and an art gallery, an independent cinema and various 'cultural enterprises' were all eventually located there. It is still evolving and developing and is now dominated by the huge and impressive buildings of the National Centre for Popular Music.

Dan Sequerra became the Director of DEED in 1985. He describes the beginnings of the Cultural Industries Quarter: '…82/83, he [Paul

Skelton, a leading member of the Employment Department staff] was dealing with young kids wanting to play music. There was not much work out there, practising in pubs and people's backrooms and…all this orientation was towards…an emerging culture which could have had a distinctive Sheffield – I know that at the time with ABC and Human League and all that …there was an attempt to brand a Sheffield culture and I think its achieved a great deal.' Dan makes an extremely important point here. The Cultural Industries Quarter has built upon activity that was already taking place in the city. There was, in the 1970s, '80s and indeed in the '90s, a number of bands from Sheffield who became successful nationally and internationally. There was also a strong local basis for the development of visual arts. As we shall see, this process of building upon activity that is already present contrasts, painfully, with the council's decision to host the World Student Games a few years later.

In addition to the Employment Department, another strategy, perhaps an unofficial one, was for the council to expand and maintain its own employment base. In the early 1980s the council employed approximately 36,000 people and was easily the city's largest employer. Peter Birch stated: '…by expanding the local authority workforce… they actually tried to cushion the effect of the massive loss of steel and engineering jobs, and certainly a lot of people I know, who'd worked in engineering, *did* move into jobs in ' city council…but the people I've named [Blunkett and Betts] would probably deny that they ever, politically, took that decision but …that's my perception.' In fact, Clive Betts did actually admit that this was the case: '…indeed by sustaining the council's own job base in terms of employment of people in housing, education, social services – that was another way of counteracting the job losses in the private sector…' Helen Jackson, who became chair of the Employment Department in 1984, also recognized the importance of the council as an employer – '…we argued, David [Blunkett] and I, particularly that what a local authority could do with its very wide remit and wide powers is recognize the place and position that the local authority played in a city or region as the largest employer, the largest economic unit, turnover of nearly a billion pounds a year, employing 36,000 people, biggest building force…biggest everything…and put that economic power and influence to use in as wide a way and most constructive way we could.'

This strategy of sustaining a large workforce met with a lot of opposition – from local business leaders, from within the council and from some of the electorate. It was felt that the council was creating jobs for their own sake, not 'real' jobs but merely employment to avoid unemployment. This was indeed the case and when, in the mid 1980s, rate-capping was applied, the council was forced to make large numbers of people redundant, and this continues to be the case right up to the present day.

One of the most important aspects of the city council's approach to economic regeneration is that it changed political direction somewhat in the early 1980s. After the initial flurry of activity – mainly the creation of the Employment Department with its emphasis on the creation of worker co-operatives, and then Bill Michie's departure to parliament in 1983 – the ideological direction of the council shifted. Clive Betts told the story: 'If you ask the people that were involved in the private sector, they would say one of the things that triggered off a closer relationship was that in 1983 we had a first visit to Ansham, which is our twin city in China, and we invited the Chief Executive of the Chamber of Commerce to come with us, which was a bit like an olive branch, given the rows that had been going on to that day. I got sat in the car with him – its just that things went in pecking order and David Blunkett was there and the deputy leader of the council, and I was sort of third or fourth councillor on the trip and the Chamber of Commerce man was, sort of, at my level, in the Chinese hierarchy of things. We got sat in the same car and we got talking about things and …out of that we began to move a bit closer together…' This, in fact, was the beginning of the City Council entering into the much-celebrated so-called 'partnerships' with the private sector. A number of the interviewees referred to these partnerships in very positive ways. In fact, the story that Clive Betts told was repeated to me by two other interviewees! It seems that it has entered local mythology!

A very brief description of the nature of these 'public-private' partnerships is required here. The council has, over the years since the mid-1980s, entered into a number of 'trusts' with the private sector and with other public bodies such as the universities or the health authority on specific projects. However, before this became possible, council and business leaders had to start communicating with each other. A series of forums were established for this purpose. The first of these was the Sheffield Economic Regeneration Committee, which was set up in 1986. This concentrated upon the regeneration of the Lower Don Valley and the building of Meadowhall Shopping Centre. This was the beginning of the so-called 'partnership' strategy.

Peter Horton, Chair of Education from 1967 to 1983 and Lord Mayor in 1987, was the most enthusiastic interviewee on these partnerships: 'I've always been involved in different sorts of partnerships – for twenty or thirty years, so I ...[am] very favourable to partnerships... private-public, or semi-public...' He went on: '...it was about the mid 80s when it began...it takes time even when you've started it... I think now its the liaison committee...a committee of the leaders...its been called other names before then...a top-level group, then there are all sorts of different partnerships for different projects...The theme that I took [as Lord Mayor] was Working Together...it had started before then, I simply took that theme...meaning that I was going to carry on working together, attend breakfast meetings...' Peter described how he favoured the adoption of such partnerships rather than the radical strategy of Blunkett's leadership. On the issue of the attitudes of some councillors to the creation of the Employment Department, he said: 'There was a feeling that radical people, if you like...were in control of it...can we afford to keep having it...some would say, its very necessary ...but is it the job of local government? ...other forms ....partnerships...to do that job...mainly on the side that was a bit sceptical ...'

Both Blunkett and Betts described the period as if there was a seamless transition from the radical, socialist politics of the early 1980s through to the adoption of partnerships with the private sector. Blunkett said: 'My only regret is that I didn't do what we did later which was to unite the whole of the city in presenting one common face.' This phrase 'the whole of the city' unites the employers (or capitalists) and the labour movement under one banner: that of Sheffield. Blunkett and many other interviewees present the idea, either directly or by inference, that Sheffield capitalists and the labour movement were, and still are, united in struggle against a common enemy. But what or who was that common enemy? It could not have been the Conservative government because many interviewees acknowledged that the people they were going into partnership with were Tories. In a very general sense, it was the forces of international capitalism which were destroying the economic and employment base in Sheffield. Thus, Blunkett et al were, in effect, making an emotional appeal to the people of Sheffield – capitalists, workers, unemployed and everyone else – to come together to save Sheffield from the worst ravages of this destruction.

There is clearly a contradiction here. These local Labour politicians described themselves as socialists and Blunkett and Green's pamphlet of 1983 clearly laid out their ideological position and the place for the private sector in it. These partnerships, which often take the form of trusts with the private sector, really do represent a complete reversal of the council's former stance, which in fact only lasted for about four or five years. The early embrace of 'municipal socialism' necessarily involved a degree of conflict with the private sector. Its anti-capitalist rhetoric created ill-feeling in local capitalists who were, they felt, being asked to pay too high a level of business rates to the council. The pamphlet, *Building from the Bottom* by Blunkett and Green (1983), refers to 'Harnessing the private sector' as point four out of five points on 'A Local Economic Strategy'. It makes no reference to partnerships with the private sector but instead mentions the following: '…we must plan and implement a long term strategy which harnesses private to public enterprise or creates partnership within the public sector.'[134] The council's whole approach, up until 1983, emphasized the tremendous importance of the public sector, not just in its traditional role of provider of such services as housing, social services and recreation but also, very importantly, as a key player in the local economy. Initially this was perceived of in an interventionist manner but later it was reduced to the council's role as an employer. This volte-face to embracing collaboration with the private sector will be examined in more detail later in the chapter. For now, it will be noted that for four or five years the council embarked upon an experiment in 'municipal socialism' before turning to the private sector to bail it out.

While a great deal of activity was taking place on the issues of employment and culture within the council, the South Yorkshire County Council was gaining a very good reputation for its transport policy. Alan Jones explained: 'Well, we'd been working towards a cheap fares policy for quite a lot o' years, in this area, and everybody was aware, when they went on 'oliday, outside o' Sheffield, how expensive bus fares seemed to be, in comparison to Sheffield. I think the benefits…were quite evident. It enabled people to get to work cheaply, families to communicate a lot easier, mothers with young kids to get on a bus and meet their grandma and so on. It kept the contact with the old and young people, it allowed the young kids to get out to pursue leisure activities – at a cheap rate.' He adds: '…in fact the 1981 Labour Party manifesto… included a commitment to working towards a *free* transport system in South Yorkshire, a *free* bus fare system.' It should be noted that the county of South Yorkshire includes the towns of Barnsley, Doncaster and Rotherham as well as Sheffield. The cheap fares policy was introduced in 1973 at the inception of the County Council.

For the population of Sheffield cheap bus fares were synonymous with the County Council and, importantly, the City Council also received a lot of credit for the policy even though transport was not within their remit. The transport policy was a practical application of the municipal socialism approach that was being expounded by Blunkett et al and people, at that time, were actually proud to belong to what had become known as 'the Socialist Republic of South Yorkshire'. Not surprisingly, Blunkett and Barton both had an involvement in the cheap fares policy; Blunkett as a County Councillor during the 1970s and Barton as a member of the County Party that decided upon the policy. The cheap fares policy was a very big success for the local Labour Party. However, in 1985 rate-capping, imposed by central government, massively restricted the ability of the County Council to maintain it. The government had already introduced deregulation of transport services which meant that private companies were able to compete with the local authority to provide transport. Bus fares had already started to increase in South Yorkshire in 1986 when the metropolitan authorities, including South Yorkshire County Council (and the GLC in London) were abolished. The abolition of the County Council got rid of the cheap fares policy and transport fares in South Yorkshire are now comparable with fares across the country.

Another event that added to Sheffield City Council's reputation as a radical, socialist local authority was its conflict over rate-capping with the Conservative government. In 1984, the council, along with a number of other local authorities including the London boroughs of Greenwich, Lambeth, Islington, Southwark and Lewisham and Liverpool City Council, decided to defy the government over the implementation of rate-capping. One of the problems, though, was that there were two different strategies being advanced by the rebel authorities. The first was outright refusal to set a rate. The second was to set the maximum legal rate and then to ignore it and overspend; a so-called 'deficit budget' approach. In fact, divisions over these two strategies caused some conflict between those authorities involved. Lambeth and Liverpool were urging outright defiance and refusal to set a rate. This strategy was eventually adopted by the whole group. One problem with this route was that individual councillors could be surcharged and this caused a great deal of panic and fear in some councillors. Alan Wigfield, who was Chair of Housing from 1986 to 1992 and Chief Whip from 1987 to 1992 on Sheffield City Council, was a member of the management committee of the organisation that was set up by the local authorities that were defying the government on rate-capping. Along with David Blunkett, who chaired it, he was Sheffield's representative. He recalled: '...you could see people were fearful. They didn't want to break ranks...they were frightened of being surcharged. I was a whip at the time – I remember the discussions – people being advised – well if you've got a house you could lose it... if we'd set a rate, then ignored it, they couldn't have done much about us really.' Council after council began to set a rate under pressure of being surcharged. Alan described the outcome in Sheffield: 'It split the Labour Group not exactly down the middle – but about twenty of the beggars went off the side and voted with the Tories to set a rate. They were stripped of their chairs of committees and things but it was clear it was gonna happen. ... It split three ways in the end. And I joined that middle group 'cos at that stage we were making bloody gestures ... we hadn't got the votes, we were making gestures...' The 'middle group' of which Alan speaks supported the 'deficit budget' approach. The campaign failed and had the effect of splitting a Labour Group that had not experienced any major cleavages almost since it first gained power in 1926. These splits were to have major ramifications later with the departure of some prominent councillors.

A very big council initiative which did not emanate from within the Employment Department was the hosting of the World Student Games. The words 'sport' and 'culture' are often linked in local authority literature and one might be forgiven for concluding that they were both part of an integrated strategy for economic regeneration of the city. However, this was not the case, as Roger Barton stated: 'Sport wasn't on the agenda – what was on the agenda was building a partnership (with the private sector) – we'd identified us priorities and us recovery plan – and we would go for it... Along came this World Student Games event and it was Gerry Montgomery, one of the officers in ' Recreation Department who came to us and…[said] we can, with correct planning, market it, turn it into a media event and as a consequence of that, not get money for television coverage, but draw in big sponsors, because we were guaranteed to get television coverage. So, Gerry infected one or two of us with his enthusiasm…' So, the origins of Sheffield hosting the World Student Games came from a member of the Recreation Department staff. Other interviewees also support this version of the events. The World Student Games made a loss of £10 million, according to Clive Betts, or £28 million according to Pat Heath.

What is very important here is that the decision to host the World Student Games was not made on the basis of building upon local sporting activity. Rather it was almost literally 'plucked out of the air' as an idea to cement the relationship between the council and the private sector and to attempt to give Sheffield an international profile. Clive Betts said something very similar: 'I think that we probably looked for a niche that nobody else had taken at that time, that we thought had potential for improving facilities for people in the city but also gaining some international attraction, gaining international events. Showing the city had a more outward looking view – that it also could get international publicity from events that came to the city. Also that it brought the public and private sectors together – cos the private sector were equally enthusiastic as the council was – and that was right the way through – it was a joint strategy. It was the first example…'

The decision to go ahead with the World Student Games met with a lot of opposition from within the council. Blunkett described himself as a 'sceptic' while Helen Jackson was completely opposed to the idea. So was Bill Michie but he, like Blunkett, was an MP by then. But the really vociferous opposition came from a group of councillors, including Helen Jackson, who consistently voted against the proposal. Pat Heath explained the nature of his, and others, opposition: '…priorities in Sheffield didn't ought to be swimming pools and running tracks, if that meant the reduced emphasis on community provision and support to disadvantaged sections in increasingly desperate parts of Sheffield…in an ideal world, you'd have circuses as well as everything else – but if its a choice between bread or circuses, you got to have bread first. And, to me it seemed obscene and immoral that you'd be sacrificing twenty-eight million quid of revenue support to finance the facilities…which is what is happening, for god knows how many years, and at the same time as basic services were having bits chopped off them – in education, social services, even in recreation. The same outfit that was inspiring everybody with talk of big swimming pools, increasingly had a job maintaining the parks and sports pitches available for local people. It just doesn't stack up.' Alan Wigfield was also firmly opposed to the World Student Games: 'What I did have the sense to see was that the World Student Games would be a disaster. Another big project…building all these sports facilities, all at the same time. And the payback – it's paying off the lease of the land…it's not this extravaganza itself, it's paying off the lease on all those sports facilities – which we'll be paying for in Sheffield for the rest of my life and beyond…For me the issue was…paying back the capital costs…'

Perhaps the most important aspect of the decision to go ahead with the games was that it was made within the context of a much reduced overall budget, due to rate-capping, and that it necessitated cuts in basic services such as housing, social services and education to finance it. It is estimated that from 1986–87 onwards the average annual cut in the council's expenditure was approximately £10 million.[135] It was this that fuelled much of the strong opposition to it, within the council and outside it. Peter Birch stated: 'I personally, and I'm sure it's shared by a lot more people in Sheffield, don't want to see an international swimming pool in ' middle o' city. What I want for my personal needs, for the needs of my grandchildren is local, community-friendly swimming baths. And local community libraries and things of that nature and we seem to have gone from shuttin' them down…what I find extremely annoying is I've got an Olympic size swimming pool that int any good for me taking a two and three year-old grandson and granddaughter – I wanna go to somet that's user friendly and I can't because my local baths at Woodthorpe have shut down…' In fact, Peter is right to suggest that many people would agree with him. A number of the other interviewees echoed this concern.

However, the actual situation is much worse than the mere closure of swimming baths, because the housing repairs budgets, the basic social services budgets and the education budgets have all been severely reduced because of the games. There was not the opportunity to interview someone directly affected by these cuts but Alan Wigfield, Chair of Housing at the time, had something to say: 'They're (Parson Cross and Arbourthorne – two very large council housing estates) a disgrace – absolutely appalling… Its dreadful…' He was equally eloquent on the subject of social services cuts: 'I wasn't particularly keen on public money going in to the cultural quarter…particularly at a time when basic services were being drastically reduced – and that was the nub of it all…suddenly…in my last two years…was how we'd, in the 80s, done away with home help charges but suddenly pensioners were finding out that they'd got to pay for the home help again. At the same time as the local authority were puttin' funds into a cultural quarter which didn't make sense to me. Here we've got estates which, like Parson Cross for example, clearly run down and needing investment, and £19 million capital receipts had been stolen in my view. To help pay off the cost of the World Student Games facilities.' It is actually impossible to describe here the extent of the social misery caused by these cuts; it will merely be noted that Sheffield's hosting of the World Student Games led directly to cuts in the basic provision of services to some of the most deprived people in the city.

One local initiative that the council is not usually associated with but, it appears, may have initiated, is the Meadowhall Shopping Centre in the mid-1980s. Helen Jackson said, in response to a question regarding the initial motivation for Meadowhall: 'I remember the argument, our Chair of Finance, Alan Billings, and David Skinner, the Chair of Planning at the time went over to Canada, on a big trip to look at shopping malls. And came back very starry-eyed about shopping malls…' Meadowhall is a huge indoor shopping centre which is built in the Lower Don Valley (along with the Don Valley Sports stadium and Arena concert venue), an area that used to be home to a large number of steel and engineering companies. The council, and then later the Sheffield Development Corporation, had a huge part to play as regards reclamation of the land, environmental improvements and identifying the potential for investment in new industries. However, their involvement in the building of Meadowhall, other than providing initial planning consent, was minimal. The whole venture, and it was a multi-million pound one, was financed by the private sector and is a very impressive example of a new, modern indoor shopping centre. The big problem is that because it was built out of town it took huge swathes of business away from Sheffield City Centre, to the extent that during the early 1990s the centre resembled a ghost town. It is estimated that the reduction in trade in the city centre was 20% by the end of the second year of Meadowhall's trading.[136] The council has now begun to address this problem, but again, as with a number of other initiatives, it failed to predict the negative consequences of some of its actions.

This leads on to yet another very large initiative that the council, in collaboration with the other councils in South Yorkshire, embarked upon in the late 1980s: the South Yorkshire Supertram. Again, very large amounts of money were involved, again, as with the World Student Games, in partnership with the private sector. The Supertram was opened in 1994 with a great deal of local publicity and civic pride. In fact, Sheffield City Council had plans for a city-wide single form of transport as early as the late 1960s, and had flirted with the idea right throughout the next two decades. When asked about Supertram, the main response from interviewees was, as Terry Gardner said: '…I've never been on it, because where I live…it wunt be goin anywhere…that's one o' arguments against it…where does it go to?' This reflects the overwhelming response of people in Sheffield: unless you live on the very restricted route of the Supertram, it is highly unlikely that you will use it. It services the city centre and Meadowhall but only from a very small part of the rest of the city. Again, perhaps the Supertram represents another example of lack of foresight on the part of the council. The other major criticism is that all the other constituent council's in South Yorkshire have had to contribute towards financing it, yet it is situated solely in Sheffield! During its construction large parts of the city, particularly the roads, were subject to extensive and prolonged disruption and therefore inconvenience to both road users and pedestrians.

Taken together, the World Student Games and Supertram are often presented by a hostile local media and others as financial 'adventures' that the city council simply could not, and cannot, afford. This is Alan Wigfield's, and other councillors', basic argument. The council is embarking upon large, high-profile and expensive initiatives at a time when it is failing to provide adequate basic services.

The story of the city council undertaking these huge initiatives is not yet over. The latest venture, largely in response to the running down of the city centre already mentioned, is the *Heart of the City* project. Again, this is a multi-million pound initiative – the council estimates £120 million – which involves building an extensive structure housing a Millennium Gallery and Winter Garden in the centre of the city. The council insists that the project will not cost the council taxpayer anything and that it is funded by the National Lottery, the European Regional Development Fund and other sources. However, the project involves the demolition of a local authority building and the destruction of a Peace Gardens and extensive building work in the city centre. There is a large amount of disruption and inconvenience to people in the city, particularly those wishing to use council services, and it is perceived by the people of Sheffield as the same type of disruption as that caused by the construction of the Supertram.

The final big initiative to mention is the winning bid in 1998 to house the United Kingdom Sports Institute. A number of the politicians who supported the hosting of the World Student Games feel vindicated by this success. In fact, David Blunkett, as Secretary of State for Education and Employment, helped the bid substantially. As he said: 'I did pull all the stops out to get the UK Institute for Sport. There's no question, had Labour not been elected, it would probably have gone to one of the other two bidders. But Richard Caborn and I made a partic-ular case for the economic importance to the city, given that Upper Heyford and the Nottingham-Loughborough bid were both in areas of very high employment.' The successful bid has generally been welcomed. However, the main critical response is, as eloquently stated by Peter Birch: '…we're gonna have all these worldwide sportsmen comin – an I think about kids on ' Manor Estate (the most deprived council estate in Sheffield) – how many o' them 'll be goin down and 'ow many o' them will be avin' opportunity to enter athletics…I seem to think that we're creating…wonderful places for rich kids to come and participate in sport and we can have the periphery jobs selling 'ot dogs or a temporary job selling tickets on a turnstile…'

To sum up, the City Council, along with a number of other bodies and organisations, has taken several initiatives over approximately the last eighteen years which, in various ways, can be said to be responses to the decline of steel production and engineering as the main economic activ-ities, in terms of providing employment. Under the general banner of economic regeneration, the Council created the Employment Department in 1981, which eventually spawned the successful Cultural Industries Quarter and the National Centre for Popular Music. It expanded its own workforce in the early 1980s, and entered into a large number of partnerships with the private sector from 1986 through to the present day. South Yorkshire County Council had a highly successful cheap fares policy until it was abolished in 1986, and it 'took on' central government directly in the mid 1980s in the bitter conflict over rate-capping. In partnership with the private sector the City Council hosted the World Student Games in 1991, supported the building of Meadowhall in the late 1980s, and, in collaboration with the other councils of South Yorkshire and the private sector, constructed the Supertram. It won the bid for the United Kingdom Sports Institute in 1998, and is currently working on the Heart of the City project. Finally, again in partnership with the private sector, it built the Sheffield Airport. It seems quite an impressive list.

What should be added to it is the idea that there is now a diverse economy in Sheffield, of which leisure, sport and culture are just one strand. Mike Bower, the leader of Sheffield City Council from 1992 to 1998, has stated this, and David Blunkett said something very similar: 'I've been very keen indeed to ensure that there was a pluralistic approach, that people saw the development of sport, and related activity including the UK Institute for Sport, and the cultural development, including the Cultural Industries, as a strand in a totality rather than ...themselves ...' He was particularly keen to stress '...the potential for the development of the very substantial investment that's gone into medical research at the University, the teaching hospitals, and the potential there that could link in with some of the other developments...the development of medical technology – something that could be a real winner, we are only at the edge of what's been done in the United States with medical technology, non-invasive surgery ...' Clive Betts was more aspirational than factual: 'I think having one or two strings to the bow, for economic development, isn't enough – you've got to have a number of ways – one thing that we ought to have learned from the past is that relying on one or two industries is the worst thing we can do, so we don't want to get too reliant on sport or leisure or tourism, so we want other things as well, for trying to have a bit of inward investment, trying to look at maybe a growing manufacturing sector which we could tap into. It would give that bit more variety and surety against the failure of any one sector in the future.'

The effects on employment in the city

Despite all this, the main questions, given that we are looking here at responses to the loss of jobs in the city, must be – how many and what type of jobs have been created by all these, and other, initiatives?

Because of the large number of variables the actual number of jobs created is very difficult to quantify. However, Kostas Georgiou, who undertook the research that supported the successful submission from

South Yorkshire for European Union Objective One Status in 1998, found that during the last twenty years 177,000 jobs were lost and in the same period the service sector provided 47,000,[137] a net loss of 130,000.

Another approach is to look at the level of unemployment, comparing it with the national picture, over the same period – approximately the last twenty-five years. In 1975 unemployment in Sheffield was approximately 2%. By 1981 it had risen to 8%, with 38,000 people unemployed. 1986 represents the high-point, with nearly 17% of the workforce out of work. This steadily fell until 1990 and rose again to approximately 12.5% of the workforce in 1992.[138] This trajectory roughly approximates to the national picture. However, until 1982 Sheffield's level remained below the national average but, very importantly, has stayed well above it ever since. The new jobs in Sheffield appear to have been created mainly in the second half of the 1980s. However, this also corresponds with the national situation so it is very difficult to interpret it in exclusively local terms. Also, during this period the government changed the method of determining the level of unemployment a number of times, so this may not be a satisfactory guide to actual levels of unemployment.

However, it is possible to be much clearer about the answer to the second question: what types of jobs have been created in Sheffield? These are overwhelmingly in the service sector, many of them in the retail sector of Meadowhall. By 1989, 65% of employment was in the service sector compared to 57% in 1981 and 44% in 1971.[139] No doubt this proportion increased in 1990 with the opening of Meadowhall. Most of the jobs created are low-paid, many of them are part-time, most are unskilled or partly-skilled and offer little job security. Kostas Georgiou found that in the twenty years between 1978 and 1998 average earnings in South Yorkshire fell from above the national average to 12% below it.[140] Trade unionism is virtually non-existent in these new jobs. Employment of women has increased significantly whilst unemployment has primarily affected men. It was this issue that inspired Simon Beaufoy to write the script for *The Full Monty* film! Thus, a 'casualized', low-paid, much-reduced, predominantly female workforce has replaced one which had a high proportion of highly-skilled, predominantly male, workers, producing high-quality and often world-famous products with very strong trade unions and concomitantly high wages.

This leads us on to the oft-repeated notion that 'Sheffield is now producing more steel than ever'. As already stated, all of the senior politicians said this. For example, Roger Barton: 'We are now manufacturing more steel in Sheffield than ever…', Clive Betts: '…it still produces more steel than it did in the late 1940s.' and Helen Jackson: '…we produce more steel now than when you were first talking about it…'. There was one dissenting voice to this 'chorus', that of Alan Wigfield: 'I'm *sickened*…of hearing people, who these days are…government ministers saying there's more steel produced in Sheffield naa than there was in its heyday. *That's absolute nonsense. Its not true at all.*'

The key issue is that while more steel than ever before may or may not be currently produced, *steel-production and engineering are providing employment for a tiny number of people compared to previously.* Between 1971 and 1993 the total numbers of people working in steel production fell from 45,100 to 4,700 – from 16% to 2% of the total workforce.[141] This simple fact makes Helen Jackson's suggestion that: '…actually the wealth of the city does still depend on the manufacturing…' seem somewhat absurd. If huge profits are being made in manufacturing in Sheffield, those profits are accruing to the capitalists and to the capitalists alone. The large majority of the population of Sheffield does not receive any benefit whatsoever. It is incidental to them. Thus, the mantra, 'more steel is currently being produced etc.', seems somewhat hollow and an affront to the people of Sheffield.

One of the issues that has not been examined in any depth in this case study is that of the social effects of high unemployment on the population of Sheffield. The interviewees who did refer to this generally agreed that the city has experienced a massive increase in crime and drug abuse. Alan Jones said: '… its taken a lot of self-respect and esteem away from people – they know they're gonna have to be on benefits and they can't plan for the future. They know that they can't do the things that twenty-five years ago were the accepted things at certain stages in your life. That, then causes all the social problems that you've mentioned – you get people fallin aat and domestic violence, neighbour disputes…my lad when he was in that situation he didn't get up till three o'clock in ' afternoon, they cum in all 'ours o' night. They become alienated, they 'av no respect for other people… So, you've got the deprivation, the unmarried mothers, the thieving, car crime, drug-taking – that's rife at the moment – its the release intit – if you've got no hope and somebody offers you a little packet o' somat, for next to nowt, which is what they do initially – then get you hooked, then to feed your habit you're having to resort to crime to fuel it. So you've got that aspect which is rife in Sheffield.' Clive Betts stated, in response to a question on the easy availability of drugs on Parson Cross council estate: 'Yes, and I think that has grown *a lot* in the last 10 years... I was councillor for Firth Park until 1992, which is the next ward on to Parsons Cross, the bottom end of Parsons Cross is in it, and think there's been a change even since that time...I think its partly the cycle of lots of unemployment in one area, low wages, people steal for their money for drugs, crime goes up, drugs are seen as a way of escaping the general problems of life and one way you can have a good time...because there's nothing else to do.'

Labour's electoral record in Sheffield since 1973

Possibly the most important way of evaluating the success of Labour's political response to the decimation of steel and engineering is to examine their electoral record during the period in question. However one looks at it, it is not much short of disastrous. Between 1973 and 1992, the Labour share of the vote fell from 57% to 38%! In 1973 Labour had sixty-nine out of a total of ninety seats.[142] After the election of May 1998, Labour had only fifty seats, while the Liberal Democrats increased their seats to thirty-six.[143] In that same election, the council leader, Mike Bower, who had been leader for the previous six years, lost his seat to a concerted Liberal Democrat campaign.

Virtually every interviewee said that they thought that the Liberal Democrats would win control of the council at the next election, or possibly the one after. It might be appropriate, therefore, to finish this section with a quote from David Blunkett on the subject of the Liberal Democrats taking over the council: 'That'd be very sad – 'cos the bad times are *fading* and it's just at that moment when people are remembering the bad times, when they need to see what's just over the horizon... Sheffield's on the verge of a renaissance and my colleagues on the city council have just got to get that message across very hard at the same time as delivering some very basic services.'

Sheffield as an illustration of labourism

The second part of this chapter will draw attention to the character-istics of labourism that are illustrated by the Sheffield case study: absence of ideology, a confused approach to policy-making, pragmatism over principles, the party's disingenuous emotional appeal, and its culture of defeatism. The characteristics not examined here are the national/sectional contradiction, since this is clearly not relevant when looking at a local party and movement, and lack of democracy. As we have seen, generally the party and movement in Sheffield were very democratic for most of the period under examination. A possible excep-tion to this could be the volte-face of the leaders of the council in the mid-1980s but since we do not actually know the extent to which this was sanctioned by the local movement, this would be mere speculation.

The Sheffield labour movement was built upon the industries of cutlery, steel production and engineering, yet, as we have seen, when faced with the massive reduction, and possible destruction, of its own economic base the trade union responses were, very surprisingly, weakness, procras-tination and passivity. Apart from the three-month-long national steel strike and a relatively small number of local disputes, the trade unions appeared to be powerless to prevent redundancies and closures. This raises the vital question: is it possible for the labour movement to affect such processes? If they had adopted another strategy could they have, at the very least, ameliorated the worst effects of the decline of manufacturing? These questions obviously are not exclusive to Sheffield. They clearly apply to the labour movement as a whole. In attempting to answer them, the very nature of British labourism itself needs to be examined.

Absence of ideology, a confused approach to policy-making and 'pragmatism' over principles

The characteristics of the absence of ideology, lack of a stated purpose and therefore the pursuit of 'pragmatism' are well illustrated in the case study. While, obviously, the Sheffield labour movement developed to represent the interests of labour in the city, the lack of specification of those interests and the nature of that representation meant that, when faced by a major economic and political challenge, it was almost completely powerless. The trade unions, despite some valiant efforts, were virtually annihilated. Adoption of such practices as short-time working is

hardly a satisfactory overall response to such a major crisis. The technological determinism of the representatives of the ISTC is no less feeble.
However, the Labour Party, mainly through control of Sheffield City
Council, appeared to present a vision and purpose that seemed to be
lacking in the industrial section of the movement. In the early 1980s,
inspired by a new, young and dynamic leadership, the Labour Group on
the council embarked upon a series of initiatives intended to combat the
worst social effects of the decline of manufacturing in the city. They also,
at the same time, sought to rid the party of the paternalist practices of the
previous generation of Labour politicians. This last aim is ably argued in
the Blunkett and Green (1983) pamphlet.

The economic and political histories of Sheffield at this time are often
perceived and presented as two different stories. The first charts the
decline of manufacturing and the trade unions' responses. The second
concentrates on the internal battles of the Labour Party: the defeat of the
'old guard', particularly in a key parliamentary election in Brightside in
1974;[144] the election of David Blunkett as leader of the council in 1980
and the adoption of a new, dynamic approach to economic regeneration
and social strategy. However, the two stories are directly linked. The
decline of manufacturing weakened the power of the old guard in the
Sheffield labour movement. The processes, so well described by Roger
Barton early in this chapter, of the trade unions throwing up men who
then became political representatives were weakening because the trade
union base itself was weakening as a result of the devastation of manufacturing industry. Barton himself said so: 'What happened then, was
that at the same time that you got the decimation of the industrial base,
in Sheffield, and all the feed-through that you'd historically had started
being starved. There were fewer people in industrial employment, those
who were there were under great pressure with threats of redundancy,
which after a while reduced the amount of trade union activity and that,
in turn, starved us of new people coming through, like the Caborns and
Michies and the Bartons or whatever – we'd been recruited as young kids.
Young kids coming in weren't being recruited in the same way because
a lot of trade unionists had either been weeded out in redundancy
targeted, myself included, or they were having to play a much lower
profile, so when they were trying to recruit, the kids were saying "just a
minute, I don't want to get in the danger zone".'

The paternalism of the old guard was, in fact, an intrinsic element of the Sheffield labour movement. The strict hierarchy of the factory was replicated within the movement. This was not only the case within the trade unions but also within the Labour Group on the council. It was the practice of the group that a newly elected councillor had to serve an 'apprenticeship' period on the council before he or she was allowed to speak in full council meetings. The break down of the feed-through process that Roger Barton refers to above created an opportunity for a new type of political approach within Sheffield labourism. The group of people who seized the opportunity were committed to a bottom-up, anti-paternalist approach precisely because of the paternalism of the previous generation of local Labour politicians. A huge problem was that they did not understand that this paternalism was an essential element of local labourism. Thus, they spectacularly failed in their mission to rid it of the paternalistic approach and thereby empower the people of Sheffield. A good example of this failure was provided in an anecdote by Alan Wigfield, the Chair of Housing: '...the move towards decentralization. We never quite succeeded. The housing department decentralized but unfortunately it was decentralized in a way that it decentralized manage-ment but not decisions. So, you had all these officers dotted all over – area offices. It was area-based management, rather than decentralization. So, what happened was you'd got loads and loads o' tenant's reps. attending meetings but I described them at the time, and still do, as a group o' tenant's reps. who were de facto managers. They'd all turn up with their patent leather briefcases, talking housing department speak and talking about tenants in the same disparaging way that officers might talk about them. They were tenant's association reps. – and they were schooled in it. Reports are produced in housing department speak, tenant's reps. get into this speak, members had got briefcases, officers had got briefcases, tenant's reps. needed briefcases...mushroomed all over the bloody shop and it was the very thing that we were looking *not* to have.' It appears that while the councillors had the political will to decentralize and empower, this essen-tially did not occur. In trying to answer the question 'why?', the limits of labourism seem again to suggest themselves. As regards the example of housing, council housing officers and the users of council housing services had become socialized into carrying out communication and transactions in a particular manner. This generally assumed that the council officers were 'experts', or at the very least had degrees of power and control over the allocation of resources. The tenants were then placed in a position of subservience: they were appealing to the officers for a share of those scarce resources. When a system of tenant representation was introduced, as part of a decentralization experiment, the tenants' representatives assumed the role of 'expert' and power-holder, rather than representatives of their association, because they felt that they had been allowed into the inner sanctum of council decision-making and in order to legitimate this status they adopted the same manner, language (and, in this example, briefcases) as the council officers. This is only one very small example of ways in which the new leadership of the council were frustrated in their attempts to 'build from the bottom up'.

Thus, the new young councillors of the early 1980s found themselves restricted by labourist practices that had been taking place, and had become entrenched, a long time before they were born. These practices were allowed, and encouraged, to flourish precisely because the labour movement did not have a stated set of principles that supported the concept of empowerment. In the absence of a set of principles describing the purposes of the labour movement, ways of working were adopted which were borrowed from the organisation of industrial factories. The management hierarchies within factories provided the models for labour movement structures. No other models were available. This point is essential to an understanding of both the labourism of the old guard and the failure of the 'young Turks' to rid the movement of paternalism. Leaders of the labour movement were detached from the ordinary worker, despite what Roger Barton said, but they were detached in such a way that the ordinary worker respected and held in great esteem his or her leaders. This was because the very concept of hierarchy was unquestioned by the labour movement. Instead, possibly by default, the movement instilled in ordinary people respect and even reverence for hierarchy. The very fact that council leaders such as Ron Ironmonger and George Wilson (the two leaders preceding David Blunkett) had themselves once worked on the factory shop floor only added to this respect.

As regards the question of a confused approach to policy-making and the concept of pragmatism, all of the council's big projects of the late 1980s and 1990s were justified on the grounds of being 'good for the city'. It was felt that, in the absence of anything else, these projects might generate some jobs, give Sheffield a higher profile and attract investment. There was no overall strategy other than this. Clive Betts actually said that this was the case: 'I think we saw leisure and tourism developing, the city has some natural advantages in terms of its location with the countryside round about. We thought of the sporting locations with the Arena offering opportunities for classical, pop concerts...with the cultural industries quarter that began to develop – they sort of *came together*. I'm not saying it was absolutely pre-planned and organized...' In the absence of a stated set of principles, Sheffield City Council was left to do whatever it could in response to the economic devastation of the city. This comes out very strongly in the quotes below from Barton, Betts and Blunkett in the section on emotional commitment. The lack of clear principles was not the responsibility of the Sheffield Labour Party in the 1980s but rather that of the national Labour Representation Committee in 1900, and the national Labour Party in 1918 and at any subsequent opportunity it has had to articulate exactly what it stands for.

Even the left-wingers within the local party were keen to indicate that they were pragmatic enough, for example, not to oppose working with the private sector in principle, but instead to look at each case on its merits. Pat Heath said: '...each case has to be looked at and the merits...I'm pragmatic enough to accept some of that stuff,...' Alan Wigfield said: 'I'm not at all against working with capitalists...' So, pragmatism is often held up as a virtue in the Labour Party against 'dogma' and even 'ideology'. However, in Sheffield we have an example of how the pursuit of pragmatism has led to enormously damaging consequences.

The labour movement's emotional appeal

The idea that labourism successfully utilizes a strong emotional appeal to its members and supporters is undeniable in the case of the Sheffield movement. The reverential tones which Roger Barton and Dan Sequerra used when referring to the District Labour Party or some of the 'great figures' of the past is evidence of this. Almost all of the interviewees showed strong signs of an emotional commitment to the local movement. In fact, interestingly, the only interviewee who did not was Seaton Gosling, the Chair of the Black Community Forum. Seaton felt very strongly that the local labour movement had failed to represent black and ethnic minority members adequately.

This emotional commitment is particularly strong in Sheffield and has its roots in some of the issues discussed earlier: relative geographical isolation, a strong sense of belonging to, and pride in, place and a relative cultural homogeneity. People have equated these things, over generations, with support for the Labour Party, electorally and morally. Perhaps even more crucially, labourism, in its many and varied forms, became entwined with virtually all aspects of people's lives. Clearly it would be present in the workplace, but the argument being presented here is that aspects of labourist thinking and practice have extended themselves into people's social and cultural lives. The domination of the latter by working-men's clubs during the early part of the period under examination, for example, is undeniable. One very positive aspect was, and still is, the widespread prevalence of co-operation within communities. Traditional working-class communities in Sheffield, as elsewhere, displayed genuine caring and co-operation. The extent and quality of this represents something of an enigma in the 1990s and early twenty-first-century Britain. This is one very positive aspect of the culture of labourism in Sheffield and elsewhere. But the negative aspect was, and still is, the passive acceptance of one's economic and social position as inevitable and possibly even natural. The phrase 'I know my place' was not always used in an ironic manner. This acceptance of subservience is endemic in the British labour movement. All of the interviewees shared a vague commitment to 'the movement' which appeals to emotions relating to solidarity and collective action.

Another aspect of this is that while the party appears to be socially progressive it is actually quite reactionary. A good example of this is Blunkett and others presenting the partnership policies of the late 1980s as if they were continuous with the socialist policies of the early 1980s. Nationally in the late 1990s this became the art of political 'spin' with, for example, cuts to single parent benefit being presented as 'encouragement' to single parents to find work! The constant exhortation by the party to the people of Sheffield in the 1980s to 'all pull together' for the good of the city forms part of this emotional appeal.

Take the following statements from Roger Barton, Clive Betts and David Blunkett: (Barton) 'They [the World Student Games] were a manifestation of an attitude and a major project that would lift us up – instead of saying we've lost a lot of jobs – you've got to come and bring them to us – we said going for something big and making a success of it and getting volunteers committed to the success of it, getting some training in supplying goods and services and whatever were part of it and it was a statement to the world we can do things, we're not just sitting back and waiting for somebody to solve our problems for us…' (Betts): 'All I would say is, if we'd done none of those things in Sheffield, where would the city be now?' (Blunkett): '…we had to do something, sitting on our hands half-tempting the inevitable decline wasn't …an option…' All three comments are in defence of actions taken by the council in response to the decline of manufacturing. They all, very clearly, appeal to a strong sense of work ethic. The message appears to be: when faced by adversity, don't lay down and let it run over you; instead fight back with action even when you are not sure that a particular action is going to be effective. Another way of putting it would be: some action is always better than no action. This message appeals very strongly, at an emotional level, to a Sheffield population that has a massively powerful work ethic instilled in it.

So, the overall message coming from the local Labour Party to the people of Sheffield is 'Look, we are trying to do our best in extremely difficult circumstances. This is the best we can do and its certainly better than doing nothing!' However, the unfortunate fact for the Sheffield movement is that the electorate were, in ever increasing numbers in the 1990s, not accepting this message and, instead, voting for the Liberal Democrats.

The culture of defeatism

This is a very difficult characteristic to illustrate with reference to the Sheffield labour movement. The prevalence of the work ethic and pride in Sheffield meant that, at times, the local movement appeared to be committed to taking action at almost any cost rather than accepting defeat. Nevertheless, it will be argued here that, in Sheffield as elsewhere in Britain, the labour movement operated with a defeatist ethic as one of its central operational characteristics. The collapse of trade unionism in the face of economic attack on its staple industries is the starkest illustration of this. The rapidity and extent of this collapse remains something of a mystery. Its detailed examination could actually form the basis of another extensive piece of research. However, the general, over-riding impression received from the interviews and from the scant literature is that of almost total collapse. Perhaps one explanation is that individual companies made redundancies and closed at different times from the early 1970s right through to the mid-1980s, so there was little opportunity for the trade union movement to mount a concerted fight-back of the type of the Miners' Strike. However, by the late 1970s it had become apparent that the industries were experiencing something more than a temporary setback, and it might have been expected that a campaign could have been mounted at that time.

As regards politics, the defeatism is illustrated by the fact that, after a very short period of experimentation with new, radical *socialist* ideas, policies and actions, the Sheffield Labour Party 'threw in its lot' with the capitalists of the city in the form of public-private partnerships. The phrase 'if you can't beat 'em, join 'em' comes to mind here. The innovative and creative nature of the Sheffield movement's socialism of the early 1980s very much contrasts with this later capitulation to capitalism and presents the picture of an almost incredibly defeatist volte-face. For example, the whole notion of socially useful production was something that had particular potential in a city where skilled craftspeople, the use of complex machinery, precision techniques and the production of high-quality products were all part of the industrial culture. Sheffield has a history of production for the defence industry and this could, with imaginative leadership, have been turned around to produce goods that were useful to people. One company actually did change from producing armaments to manufacturing hip replacements! While the local party did flirt with this idea in the early 1980s, it came to very little. David Blunkett explained the problem: '…we were picking up what happened in the '70s with Lucas Aerospace – the real enthusiasm for trying to look at how you could use the skills of those who'd considerable experience but recognizing that what they were producing was no longer marketable…So, we were enthusiastic for this, but we were really a very small voice – the enthusiasts – we used to meet …there used to be conferences, we got the Lucas Aerospace Combine to come and talk……but there was no-one behind it …it was an interesting period in history…' The 'no-one behind it' not only included a complete lack of financial support but also any enthusiasm for the concept from the national Labour Party. The Sheffield party were left isolated in their support for socially useful production in the city. Here was a chance for the skilled engineers and craftspeople of Sheffield to use their skills and their otherwise redundant machinery to make useful products that would be bought by local people. It appears that a huge leap of imagination and intervention were required to do this, but these were simply beyond the capabilities of labourist thinking. This is a stark illustration of the essential passivity of the labour movement. The opportunity for people to earn their living by employing their skills on producing things that would be of real benefit to individuals and communities and for which, therefore, there would be a stable market, was not taken, *because of the very nature of labourism*. It is not within the remit of the latter to be pro-active and imaginative to the degree required to take advantage of this type of opportunity. Instead, the party passively accepted the economic and technological changes, ultimately with very little challenge.

A final element of the culture of defeatism will be very briefly mentioned. Labour has never been a 'hegemonizing' party and has often pandered to the ignorance and prejudices of the electorate. The recent scapegoating of single parents and asylum seekers is a good example of this. Sheffield experienced a smaller amount of post-war immigration of ethnic minority people than many other northern cities, for example Manchester or Liverpool. There is insufficient space here to look at the labour movement's responses to this immigration, which could itself be the subject of a book. Instead, some of the comments of Seaton Gosling, the current Chair of the Black Community Forum, will be cited and hopefully will speak for themselves. Seaton came to Sheffield from Jamaica in the early 1960s and worked for a company called Tinsley Wire and for British Steel. He said: 'I wouldn't say…that the trade union movement has ever been properly opened up to black people. You get representation because you're a part of the workforce, but in a lot of the cases, the representation you get is tokenism …I din't think …that has changed up to today. If you look across the country, then you might say … Secretary of the T & G, Bill Morris…but the percentage of black people in the workforce and their representation in the trade union does not reflect the percentage.' and: 'I am generally interested in the trade union movement. Because of my political feelings…if the opportunity has arisen, I would have got more involved in it…Because the opportunity wasn't there for black people in those days.' Finally: '…the trade union wasn't set up to protect your rights, in that way… it was a white structured thing and it didn't take on board that you have a lot of foreigners coming in – they didn't take that on board – that you were part of the workforce, that's you're rights needed defending.'

Conclusion – the defeat of labourism?

It would be disingenuous to suggest that all of the initiatives taken by the city council have been unsuccessful or unpopular. Clearly, the cheap fares policy of the County Council was both enormously successful and popular. Some of the other initiatives may yet prove to be as beneficial. The Cultural Industries Quarter has had some successes, although its appeal is limited to a minority of the population. The National Centre for Popular Music may prove to be the tourist attraction that they are hoping for, while the United Kingdom Institute for Sport may be the spur for attracting investment in medical technology relating to sport. However, the hosting of the World Student Games and the Supertram are very widely perceived to be major mistaken decisions that have cost the council enormous amounts of money with very little benefit. It remains to be seen whether central government will provide a significant proportion of the cost of building Supertram. At present, the Heart of the City project appears to be another major financial adventure.

There is an important distinction to be made between the Cultural Industries Quarter and the World Student Games. While the former is actually built upon the experience and activity of people within Sheffield, the latter was imposed on the city. Sport and sporting excellence were not intrinsic to the locality. Whether this makes any difference in commercial terms is not yet known. However, one can make an analogy with the development of steel production and engineering. The availability of iron ore, coal and water power locally obviously contributed to the development of Sheffield's manufacturing industries. These industries were built upon the availability of natural local resources. However, when in the 1980s the council and other parts of the labour movement were considering their next move, the idea of sporting excellence was not building upon anything other than one council officer's enthusiasm! It was a form of social engineering. But despite this, Sheffield may yet become the 'National City of Sport'.

However, the latter point is a mere quibble compared to the issue of Sheffield City Council's ideological U-turns. The period from the 1950s to the 1970s has been examined briefly and shown to be one when there was a tremendous strength and unity in the local labour movement. It appears though that this strength was actually based upon the health and strength of manufacturing industry locally. When the latter was massively reduced, the fortunes of the labour movement were reduced with it. To state it simply, it appears that a healthy capitalist economy equated with a strong labour movement. The presence of industrial subsidies from Europe also contributed to this situation. It has been argued that the trade union response to the sudden decline was passivity and helplessness. However, for a very brief period in the first half of the 1980s, under David Blunkett's leadership, the council experimented with a new form of municipal socialism that inspired many in the movement inside and outside Sheffield. It was radical, creative, innovative and exciting. It was also an attempt to put some socialist rather than social-democratic ideas into practice. Blunkett and Green (1983), in a section entitled 'The Limits of Social Democracy', argue:

Labour spokesmen in government and opposition have agreed that the wealth of this country, and in any other capitalist economy, is created by private industry and spent by the public sector. They distinguish, then, a productive private sector and a non-productive public sector. Logically, it follows from this general economic assertion that candy floss is productive, an extra stair rail for a handicapped person is not. Rubber ducks, plastic gnomes and fruit machines create wealth; council houses, school text books and wheelchairs dissipate it. Should these distinctions be too crude then a supplementary argument is brought to the rescue. No matter what the product, goods or services, its worth revolves around whether it is produced by the public or the private sector. Thus the home helps who are employed in increasing numbers by Sheffield City Council are thought to be a bad thing, if not intrinsically, then because the nation cannot afford them; whereas the Home Angels, the parallel private service for those who can afford it in the private market, are a good thing. An economic definition which is essentially social democratic in origin thus ends up supporting – or at least not denying – Conservative arguments for privatization. This underlines the need for a clear socialist analysis of production and social expenditure.[145]

Alan Wigfield, in response to a comment that the period of Blunkett's leadership was perceived of as radical, creative and innovative, enthused: 'Absolutely, I would agree entirely. It was a *wonderful* time to be a member of the Sheffield local authority. A wonderful time.' In fact, the Sheffield labour movement had a reputation for being left-wing well before the arrival of Blunkett's leadership of the council in 1980. The strong presence of the Communist Party and its influence in the Trades and Labour Council is testament to this. There is also the fact that the

Sheffield Labour Party resisted the split between the unions and party, which was a national instruction, until the last possible moment. Even then, for many years subsequently, the Trades Council and the District Labour Party continued to operate as if they were one body. As we have seen, a number of interviewees, including Roger Barton, Dan Sequerra and Alan Wigfield, stated that this was the case. There was a general acceptance that Sheffield was something of a left-wing or socialist enclave of the labour movement, despite the paternalism of the old guard.

However, it was with the arrival of the so-called 'Young Turks' in 1980, with their anti-paternalist ethic, that the idea of the Socialist Republic of South Yorkshire first began to take shape. While much of what has been reported about the city council's politics during the first half of the 1980s tends to concentrate on its rhetorical radical aspects, there was definitely a genuine will amongst a number of, predominantly younger, councillors, to adopt policies and practices that directly challenged both the paternalism of previous local Labour Party and labour movement leaderships *and* the Conservative government under Margaret Thatcher. The conclusion to Blunkett and Green (1983) begins: 'It is no accident that the Tories have chosen to launch a bitter and devastating attack on local government, and on socialist Labour councils in particular. Along with trade unions, socialism in the community provides not just a defence but a real alternative to our opponents. The Tories know that examples of community enterprise and social ownership and democracy at local level threaten their re-structuring of our economic and social relationships. To destroy socialist initiative at local level is seen by them as destroying the last areas of Labour's strength and with it the base from which to rebuild a committed socialist party with real and popular support.'[146]

Obviously this was an extremely ambitious task, particularly in view of the economic situation in which they found themselves. However, in 1983 the council embarked upon a process that was to change the nature of their project completely. The chance contact made in that year between the then leader of the council, Clive Betts, and the Chief Executive of the Chamber of Commerce in a taxi in Ansham in China, so well described by Clive earlier in the chapter, was to change the course of Labour politics in Sheffield. From then on the council went into a series of partnerships with the local private sector that were to form the cornerstone of their political project right up to the present day. The ideas for the economic regeneration of the Lower Don Valley, the

Cultural Industries Quarter, the World Student Games, Supertram, the Airport and now the Heart of the City project are all very large-scale examples of these partnerships. There are also numerous examples of smaller ones, including the rescue and management of Sheffield's industrial museums by the so-called Industrial Museum Trust.

This collaboration with the private sector had no precedent in the Sheffield movement, as stated by David Blunkett '…there hadn't been forums developed for that and it was only from 1983 onwards that we started to do that. It'd really been achieved about a year before I left – I was elected to Parliament in 1987, by 1986 we'd got quite a good set of links with the private sector…' In fact, there *had* been a type of collaboration before, with the private sector as employers and the labour movement representing employees. The industrial and political sections of the Sheffield labour movement had very ably represented the interests of workers and others during the whole period of economic boom in Sheffield. There is no question about this. However, when the local economy began to collapse, so did the strength of the labour movement. Faced by international competition, steel-producing and engineering companies either made huge redundancies, closed down or moved their operations to more profitable parts of the world. They simply no longer required the labour of the people of Sheffield.

For approximately four or five years, the local Labour Party embarked upon an experiment of municipal socialism, the most visible and courageous element of which was the creation of the Employment Department. When this appeared to be having little success, they turned to the private sector to help them out. Within the Employment Department this notion of 'partnerships', under the political leadership of Helen Jackson and the management of Dan Sequerra, began to have influence. Dan said: 'We really heralded the work on partnership that is so much in vogue now.' The notion had both a symbolic, rhetorical *and* actual value for the council. The symbolic value largely relates to 'the Sheffield factor' discussed above: Blunkett's appeal to all the people of Sheffield to come together when faced by economic crisis and potential devastation. The actual value is obvious: none of the large-scale, and not many of the small-scale, projects carried out by the council in the second half of the 1980s and 1990s would have happened without the financial support of the private sector. In that sense, the private sector 'saved' the council.

In effect, therefore, the local Labour Party, when faced by economic crisis, turned to the very forces that had 'wreaked havoc' in the first instance. It was, in essence, the forces of international capitalism that had destroyed the steel and engineering industries as sources of employment in Sheffield. After a very brief flirtation with socialist ideas and practices from 1980 to 1984-85, the local party completely threw in their lot with the remainder of the local private sector. There are two very important issues here. The first is that this rump of the private sector remained because of emotional loyalty and commitment to Sheffield. Peter Horton referred to: 'A different kind of pride in Sheffield amongst all classes of society – not least amongst the bosses, the wealthy.' This pride in place has already been examined and clearly extends to some of the wealthy people of the city. Without this somewhat frail, emotional commitment, capitalists could have abandoned Sheffield completely. The second issue is that, within the boundaries of labourist thought, the council had no alternative available to it other than collaboration with the private sector. It had attempted a brief socialist experiment which was deemed to be a failure. Labourism had no other models, or even ideas, to offer to the leadership of Sheffield City Council, other than for them to enter into agreements with the private sector.

A very important ideological point is that clearly these partnerships, by their very nature, were top-down in approach, in complete contrast to the leadership's stated determination to build from the bottom up. They involved collaboration between the business leaders and leaders of the council and did not involve people lower down the business and political hierarchies. This is the starkest illustration of the nature of the council's complete volte-face on economic and political strategy in this period.

This all too brief description of the politics of Labour in Sheffield in the first half of the 1980s provides an example of the limits of labourism. From its inception nationally the party has always had a socialist element or left-wing. Whilst its influenced has waxed and waned over the years, generally it had been a somewhat ineffectual force within the party. This also proved to be the case in Sheffield. The young leadership of the Labour Group during that period were undoubtedly socialists. Indeed, Helen Jackson said so: 'They were socialists, they had strong political principles...' They were all relatively young, very keen, highly motivated and intelligent. Both Pat Heath and Alan Wigfield were keen to point out that the left grouping on the council comprised themselves plus Helen Jackson, Bill Michie and Steve Jones. They could command the support of approximately twenty-three of the sixty Labour Group councillors during that period. Importantly, Blunkett, Betts, Caborn, Roger and Joan Barton, Mike Bower, and Peter Price all belonged to a more central grouping.

However, when the political crisis of rate-capping occurred, their strength and relative unity was broken forever. Both Pat Heath and Alan Wigfield, who had been Chair of Social Services and Chair of Housing/Chief Whip respectively, subsequently left the council and, indeed, the Labour Party in the early 1990s, in absolute disgust at the policies being pursued by the leadership.

The 'big projects' or, as Patrick Seyd (1993) refers to them, *grand projets*,[147] of the council represent a turning away from any socialist content to their policies. Indeed, while these huge, financially burdensome ventures are being undertaken in the name of economic regeneration, basic housing, social services and education budgets are being drastically cut. However skilful one might be at political spin, it is impossible to describe these measures as, in any sense, socialist. The partnerships with the private sector have been financially disastrous for the council, the most glaringly obvious example being the decision to host the World Student Games in 1991. However, it is not the abandonment of socialist policies that is of major importance here: socialist policies cannot be expected from the Labour Party. Rather it is the lack of success of the policies, even when judged solely from an electoral perspective. The sliding away of support from the Labour Party in the city has been shown, and, of all of the interviewees, only Clive Betts held out the prospect of Labour not losing the council in the next two elections. All the other interviewees thought it extremely likely that the Liberal Democrats would take over, although none of them welcomed it. Labourism is failing dramatically in Sheffield precisely when it is experiencing tremendous electoral regeneration at the national level. It is beyond the remit of this chapter to address this apparent irony in any detail. It will merely be noted that Labour's success at a national level in 1997, was dependent upon the 'time for a change' factor rather than mass support for New Labour ideology.

Apart from this apparent local/national discrepancy, there is a very real sense in which the local party mirrors the national one. Interviewees were asked if the local Labour Party could, in any sense, currently be described as 'New Labour'. Most of them while acknowledging that Bower's leadership of the City Council (until May 1998) bore some similarities to Blair's, were keen to draw a distinction between the two. However, many also noted that the council's early embrace of partnerships with the private sector was later taken up by the national party. Peter Horton said, on partnerships, 'It *was* New Labour, it wasn't called that but that's what New Labour is also about... It was an early manifestation of something that's now been taken up as New Labour. It was certainly new to the labour movement here.' Clive Betts said: '...the city is working together more as a whole now and the council is acting as a catalyst and an enabler as well as a provider of services. It does provide services but it does other things as well and works with the private sector. Nationally the Labour Party is very much into partnership – there is no doubt at all that partnership began in local government...'

However, the strongest comparisons were drawn by Pat Heath at the time. He thought that the very notion of partnerships with the private sector were: '...a bit of a joke....Private sector partnerships sounded grand but when push came to shove the private sector wouldn't even stump up money to fund the Christmas illuminations and it was all a taking exercise on their part and a giving exercise by the local authority, which is not really the spirit of true partnership, as I understand it.' On the subjects of the Cultural Industries Quarter and the World Student Games, he said: '...gloss, froth and rhetoric which is typical of the Labour Party with the emphasis on image and nothing on substance.'

This idea of the party's emphasis on image and appearance rather than substance takes us back to the disingenuous emotional appeal of the party. In Sheffield the contemporary manifestations of this appeal are the view of the City as 'the national city of Sport' and the home of the National Centre for Popular Music. Examples at a national level are the construction of The Millennium Dome, the Social Exclusion Unit and the very idea of New Labour itself. The novelty of New Labour is much more symbolic than real and appeals to members and supporters emotionally rather than rationally. In a similar manner, some people in Sheffield are now proud of the idea of the city as one of sporting excellence, cultural innovation, leisure and tourism. Labour governments, oppositions and local authorities often give the impression of doing something important while their actions are of very little actual substance. The phrase 'being *seen* to do something' seems to sum this up very well. The importance of the symbolic and emotional to labourism cannot be overemphasized. Since the mid to late 1980s, in Sheffield, as nationally, the 'big venture' has, to some extent, replaced the emotional appeal and symbolism of 'the movement' as one of the main motivating factors for supporters and members of the Labour Party. The Trades and Labour Council and later the Trades Council and the District Labour Party symbolically embodied the power of labour in much the same way as the idea of Sheffield as 'the city of sport' does today.

However, this apparent activity could not cover up what were, when it came to a crisis, deep divisions within the Sheffield labour movement. Employment in manufacturing was, during the period under examination, dependent upon two industries: specialist steel production and engineering. Initially the latter clearly developed in Sheffield because of the existence of the former. However, the nature of the two industries, and particularly the ways in which the two main unions representing each industry organized, were vastly different. The main union in the steel works was the ISTC. Until 1974 it was known as the British Iron, Steel and Kindred Trades Association (BISAKTA). In response to a question about whether the ISTC could be characterized as a 'right-wing' union Ted Thorne, an ex-Communist himself, had the following to say about the name: 'I'll tell you this – its original name was BISAKTA – British Iron and Steel Kindred Trades Association. … altered in the 70s I think…I always said because its name stank in the nostrils of the British labour movement.' Other commentators were just as forthright. There was something of a consensus, among the commentators that within the labour movement the ISTC was something of a right-wing union. There was also a consensus that, as Ted said: '…the ISTC stood aloof from other trade unions in the area.' This was also the case, generally, at the national level. There is insufficient space here to deal with the history of the ISTC, which is examined in detail in Upham (1997). However, it should be noted that the overall impression received, both from the interviewees and from the literature, is that of the relative isolation of the ISTC within the local and national labour movement. For example, the union did not get involved with the Trades and Labour Council, and later the Trades Council, in Sheffield but was actively involved in the Rotherham Trades and Labour Council. One possible explanation for this was the dominance of the AEU in Sheffield, with its very strong

Communist Party presence, a presence emphasized in both the interviews and the literature. In practice, despite their apparent differences,
when the local economy was booming the methods employed by the two
unions were very similar. Both recruited heavily and were very successful
and most companies had 100 per cent membership. Both believed
strongly in industrial discipline, in both the union and work-organisa-
tion sense. As we have seen, both unions enhanced rather than weakened
the organisation of work and workplaces.

However, when the crisis of manufacturing arrived in Sheffield, the
unions did not, in any real sense, work together. It is very difficult to
ascertain specific information on this subject as most commentators
acknowledged that the overall union response to the rapid decline was
minimal, confused and sporadic. The only proper example of an organized, or concerted, response was the national steel strike of 1980. This
will now be very briefly considered, with a view to examining the extent
and nature of inter-union co-operation. The trade unions officially on
strike were the ISTC, the NUB, the TGWU, the GMWU and the
constituent members of the NCCC, which included the AEU. The
dispute was with the British Steel Corporation and the strike was
extended, after one month, to steel companies in the private sector. The
NUR and ASLEF supported it by blocking the movement of steel by
rail. This appears, at first sight, to be an example of a dispute with all the
main unions involved worked together. However, given the nature of the
problem – an all-out attack on Sheffield's staple industries – inter-union
co-operation within the city was much less than might have been
expected. The first problem was with workers in the private steel-
producing companies. They were reluctant to strike because they
perceived that the dispute was with BSC and therefore did not affect
them, The strike was weakened by their actions. During the three
months of the action some private sector workers went on strike and
then returned to work on a number of occasions. The most notable
company was Hadfield's, probably because of its size. The closure of the
company by mass picketing was the cause of great celebration. However,
such high-points were rare and by April 1st the strike was called off. In
fact, the only areas that publicly supported continuing the strike were
Rotherham and Scotland. The unions at the large BSC plant at Tinsley
Park in Sheffield supported a settlement and return to work. The minutiae and machinations of the dispute are covered in Upham (1997). The

fact that no interviewee claimed it was a victory, and that massive job losses ensued immediately after the strike, is sufficient for the purposes of our argument.

The political differences and suspicions between the ISTC and the AEU did not appear to surface locally. However, they were clearly present at the national level and this, no doubt, affected the effectiveness of the strike. Also, because the dispute was with BSC, it would have been very difficult, if not impossible, for local union activists to extend it to a call to defend Sheffield (and Rotherham) steel as a whole. Trade unions are very bureaucratic bodies and would have found it almost impossible to campaign to defend the whole of steel and engineering . Thus the high-point of local trade union militancy – the steel strike – was focused on BSC, and the idea that it was anything other than a specific dispute existed only in the minds of the most idealistic activist. While inter-union co-operation and solidarity in Sheffield was strong, the unions always worked within the parameters of the official remit of the strike.

As for the political response to the attack on manufacturing in the city, the Labour Party, through the mechanisms of the City Council, experimented with a new form of municipal socialism for a very short period before abandoning it for an admittedly novel form of the old labourist 'deal' with the private sector. Even supporters such as Patrick Seyd (1993) acknowledge this: 'From 1985 onwards a policy reappraisal occurred in city government, perhaps best described as a shift from new socialism to new realism.'[148] This illustrates yet another aspect of labourism. The party, and movement, has always had a small element within it that is committed to socialist politics. As already suggested, its influence has increased and decreased over the years, but generally it has been relatively small and therefore ineffectual. In the first half of the 1980s the Sheffield Labour Group was explicitly socialist in its politics, and its period of power coincided with the rise of the left in national Labour politics. However, particularly after the crisis and defeat of rate-capping, the leadership of this group abandoned their socialist politics in favour of partnerships with the private sector. Instead of representing labour in the traditional arrangement with capitalists and capitalism, it went into direct partnerships with them to 'save the city'. The extent to which this has been successful is highly questionable. The city still has above average unemployment and the trend seems to be concomitant with the national situation. As already shown, there is a strong expectation that the Liberal Democrats will take control of the council within the next two years, breaking over seventy years of almost completely continuous Labour rule! Given these two factors alone, 'success' is not a word that springs to mind!

Rate-capping and the subsequent partnership policies caused an unprecedented split in the Labour Group and, after the departure of most of the leadership to Parliament and the resignation of some leading members, the group lost coherence and direction and was dispirited. Patrick Seyd (1993) supports this view: '...there was a distinct sense of demoralization and disillusion among existing councillors. Local political leadership was diminishing to the detriment of the city.'[149]

Over the period 1978 to 1998, 177,000 jobs have been lost in South Yorkshire.[150] Sheffield, as the largest city, has lost nearly 100,000 of these, the overwhelming majority in steel production and engineering. Both the electoral and economic stories of the Sheffield labour movement over the period being examined are very bleak indeed. In the twenty-five years from 1973 to 1998 the labour movement has gone from being, arguably, one of the strongest and proudest in Western Europe to, on the industrial side, being decimated and only existing in the marginal remains of manufacturing industry. Politically, it is within sight of losing control of the City Council to the Liberal Democrats. This sorry story can be accounted for almost entirely by reference to labourism's general character and nature.

In presenting my criticisms I have attempted to be respectful of the traditions, ideas and practices of the Sheffield labour movement, and the labour movement generally.[151] I have also tried to emphasize the positive whenever this has been possible. I am not consciously engaged in a 'ruthless criticism of all that exists' type of exercise and do acknowledge the enormity of the tasks faced by the movement in the period being studied. Hopefully the case study has highlighted some of the strengths of the local movement and the movement generally. Nevertheless, the critical characteristics of labourism provided earlier have been illustrated by the examples provided in the case study.

The issue of the lack of specification of purpose at the inception of the Labour Party nationally, and subsequently, has been looked at in detail in earlier chapters. However, if for nothing else, the Labour Party was created to represent the interests of labour. This is axiomatic. But after 1985 the Sheffield Labour Party was a passive observer of the economic and social decline of the city. Other than setting up partner-ships with the private sector, many of them huge and financially draining projects, they were not ideologically equipped to deal with the enormity and complexity of the problems facing the city. Clearly this criticism is not exclusive to Sheffield. The local party was part of a national party that was also floundering and, in fact, incorporating elements of Thatcherism into its political arsenal. In this sense, the chapter is not blaming the local party but rather placing its failures within the context of the failure of labourism as a whole. The Sheffield labour movement, despite its enormous strength and engagement in the community, was not equipped with the ideas and arguments that would enable it to defend the interests of the workers and unemployed people of the city. It was part of a tradition that had spurned theory and ideology over eighty years earlier and thus was left with nowhere to turn but to local capitalists who were loyal to Sheffield.

If a very strong labour movement cannot defend jobs, or even amelio-rate the worst aspects of economic crisis, then a legitimate question to ask is – 'what is its purpose?' So far this book has successfully avoided presenting a 'counter-factual history' and it will continue to do so. However, the question arises: could any body or group or organisation have defended the rights of workers in Sheffield with some degree of success, given the enormous weight of the adverse factors involved? The movement was faced by under-investment in plant, removal of subsidies from Europe, a hostile Conservative government under Mrs. Thatcher, a divided national labour movement and international economic compe-tition. Faced with this barrage could anyone or anything have done a better job of defence than the local labour movement?

It is an implicit, and indeed now explicit, argument of this book that the nature of labourism itself is responsible for the enormity of this and other defeats, and therefore that alternative approaches could have met with greater success. Fortunately this book has the luxury of character-izing and criticizing without the detailed specification of an alternative. However, the criticisms and characterization carry an implicit message that will be returned to in the final chapter.

It seems appropriate to conclude a chapter based on the thoughts and feelings of others by presenting three quotes from very different sources regarding the plight of the labour movement in Sheffield. These will summarize, more implicitly than explicitly, the overall message of this chapter. The first quote is from Bob Kerslake, the new Chief Executive of Sheffield City Council. At the beginning of an article entitled 'Sheffield. Planning for Change' in *Cross Talk*, a new newsletter produced by the council for the people of Parson Cross council estate, he writes: 'This is an exciting time for Sheffield, the Council, and the Parson Cross area. The City has had several notable successes recently, including the redevelopment of the Heart of the City and the United Kingdom Sports Institute project – not to mention the Full Monty!'[152] It is difficult to imagine that any of these things, with the possible exception of the *Full Monty* film, could raise any excitement whatsoever in the people who form the 25 per cent unemployed in the Southey Green ward of the estate.[153]

The second quote is from a catalogue piece advertising a local 'cutting-edge' art project, in the Cultural Industries Quarter, entitled *Provincially Provisionally* by Andrew Stones: 'Sheffield is among a number of regional towns and cities which emerged due to the demands of manufacturing industry, and the idea of cultural identity in these places becomes to some extent defined by that industry. Throughout the 1980s, many aspects of 20th century regional life were vigorously appropriated by a heritage industry keen to promote certain kinds of – especially working class – experience as forms of indigenous culture. Many have seen this as a cynical attempt to disguise the social effects of downsizing in manufacturing industry, often itself perceived as an attack on a particular kind of collective identity.'[154]

The final quote is from an anonymous former worker of Snow's, a company which specialized in grinding, after the factory closed in March 1981: 'A sense of fear has gone through this district. Its been a strong district for trade union organisation – when things have been more equal, or when the unions have had a little bit more power. But at this point in time they have none left, and it's a time when they should organize and come together, but in my opinion they've failed to do that. And by failing to do that, as they should have done, they've let it get worse, and now they can't make up the ground, and so there's no resistance.'[155]

Postscript

This chapter was completed early in 1999 and much has happened since then.[156]

As predicted by many of my interviewees, the Liberal Democrats did gain control of Sheffield City Council in the elections of May 1999, with a majority of seven. Whether or not they remain in power, they won a hugely symbolic victory, taking control of a council that had been Labour-run almost continuously for seventy-three years.

The name of Sheffield had been synonymous with the Labour Party and the Liberals made much play of this fact. Despite feeling distinctly uneasy about it, I essentially predict this loss of power in the chapter and attempt to explain the reasons for it. Rather than re-run them here, I will quote the words of a Sheffield elector, Rose Cowan, who had been a loyal Labour voter in Sheffield, but who voted Liberal Democrat in May 1999 because: 'Labour didn't come, didn't listen and when they did anything it wasn't 'What do you want?' but what they'd decided we should have.'[157]

On May 4th 2000 the Liberal Democrats consolidated their control of Sheffield City Council, with a further two seats gained from Labour. The current balance of power is: Liberal Democrat 49, Labour 37 and Conservatives 1.

On October 6th 1999 the United Kingdom Sports Institute, the presence of which substantiated Sheffield's claim to be the 'National City of Sport', announced that it was moving to London. Two reasons were given: companies involved with sport and sports technology simply did not want to locate in Sheffield, and it was felt that it would be cheaper for the UKSI to operate in London, with fewer staff and use of more advanced technology. Blunkett's hopes of developing medical research and technology, alongside the development of sport, have also obviously come to nothing.

On November 2nd 1999 the National Centre for Popular Music was saved from bankruptcy but its future is very uncertain. The centre had attracted only a quarter of the 400,000 visitors per year that it had anticipated. With debts of over one million pounds, a new head was employed to try to turn the centre around.

Also in 1999, the South Yorkshire Supertram was sold to the private company Stagecoach, because of financial difficulties due to insufficient numbers of passengers. For the same reason, in April 2000 Sheffield

Airport lost its link with London City Airport, just six months after the launch of the service.

In June 2000, the steel company Corus announced job cuts of 1,200 in Rotherham and Sheffield. In August 2000 Sheffield was cited as among the top ten locations for large telephone call-centres.

Unfortunately, most of these events could have been predicted on the basis of the substantive argument in this chapter.[158]

Chapter 4

Conclusion – a new

characterization of Labourism?

This book began by asking the question 'what is labourism?' and the first chapter examined a number of perspectives on the subject. That chapter suggested that these characterizations of labourism generally fail to deal adequately with the question of the effectiveness of the Labour Party and labour movement throughout its history. They also fail to explain labourism's relative and conspicuous absence as a concept in common use as compared with the concepts of conservatism and liberalism. This final chapter aims to provide such a characterization of the concept of labourism. The book has generally concentrated upon the ineffectiveness of both the movement and party throughout the last 101 years. This needs some explanation and justification.

I am not suggesting that the ideas, policies and actions of the labour movement during this whole period have been without any success. This would be both absurd and unreasonable as well as simply untrue. The creation of the welfare state, including the National Health Service, and the bringing into public ownership of large sections of manufacturing and service industries after the Second World War stand out as examples of the tremendous successes that the party has experienced during its existence. These successes are not unappreciated nor are they cursorily dismissed. However, the aim of this book is *not* to present a characterization that provides a balanced and would-be 'objective' account of the party and movement but instead one that is a critical analysis of the origins and development of that party and movement for the whole of the party's existence. Therefore the absence of a favourable treatment of many of the aspects of labourism does not imply a lack of appreciation of them. One that should be acknowledged is the tremendous, often indirect, contribution made by trade unions and the Labour Party to collective and co-operative ideologies and practical approaches to social life in Britain, particularly among those people towards the bottom of the social and economic scale. To suggest that 'working-class solidarity' expresses itself primarily in 'industrial action', as some left-wing commentators and activists do, is both misleading and untrue. The general attitudes and behaviour of 'ordinary' people when going about their daily lives have been influenced by the labour movement in numerous and varied ways of which perhaps even they themselves are often unaware. Manifestations of such things would range from a general neighbourliness and looking after one's friends and family through the development of local social and sports groups to the creation of such national institutions as the Co-operative Retail Society and the Club and Institute Union (the national federation of working-men's clubs). These type of things are undoubtedly largely attributable to a strong and vibrant labour movement in Britain. They have strong durable roots in working-class social life and are an integral part of such communities.

However, such things represent an extremely limited form of success for the movement as a whole and are, in fact, somewhat peripheral to its main aims and objectives, in so far as the latter can be discerned. The encouragement of and participation in 'community life' has periodically, and always rhetorically, appeared as a national Labour Party initiative but rarely as a central commitment, either when the party has been in opposition or when in government. Strong communities were and are a by-product of labourism. Ironically, 'community' – not surprisingly left undefined – is one of the elements of the current rhetoric of New Labour.

So, it is with the *critical* analysis of labourism that this book has been, and continues to be, concerned, and the characteristics presented may therefore appear somewhat pejorative and negative. They have, nevertheless, been developed in a context of sympathy, and a great deal of familiarity, with the modus operandi of the labour movement and Labour Party.

It could be, and has been, argued, for example by Michels (1962) in the early part of the century, that involvement in parliamentary activity by left-wing, socialist or social-democratic parties leads to them becoming parties of piecemeal social reform, rather than socialist parties – that their very taking part in electoral activity will lead to them dropping their aims of wholesale qualitative social change in favour of piece-meal reforms. While this notion may have some attractiveness as regards the development of Western European social democratic parties in the twentieth century, this book will argue very strongly against the idea that this is an automatic process. It also argues that this is definitely not rele-vant to the British Labour Party since it began life as a party of piecemeal social reform rather than becoming one as a result of bending to the pres-sures of parliamentary and governmental responsibility.

It should then be reiterated that the characterization provided here is intended to apply to the whole of the period since the Labour Party's inception in 1900 with the creation of the Labour Representation Committee. This is a period of 101 years and critics could take issue with the idea that it has remained essentially the same type of party for such a long time. It could be argued that the party has undergone a number of changes and indeed transformations such as the revisionism of the late 1950s and early 1960s, the Wilsonian 'modernization' of the 1960s and the creation of New Labour in the 1990s. It will be argued here that these developments, while by no means insignificant, do not transgress the basic character of labourism. Indeed they all – including, impor-tantly, Blair's New Labour – can be located precisely and unequivocally within the boundaries of labourism elucidated here. The nature of these boundaries will be examined later in the chapter.

Anyone wishing to suggest that this characterization is an over-simplification or over-generalization when applied to the whole of the party's existence might pause to compare the nature of the first Labour government in 1924 with that of Tony Blair in 1997. The cautiousness of both are their most striking features. The centralization of power in the hands of a very small number of people is also a very strong simi-larity. In 1924 Ramsay MacDonald, Sidney Webb, Philip Snowden, J.H. Thomas and Arthur Henderson met at Webb's house to decide upon the strategy of the government. It is worth citing Snowden's later recollections of this meeting: 'The conversation…turned upon what we might be able to do in the first session. There would be two courses open to us. We might use the opportunity for a demonstration and introduce some bold Socialist measures, knowing, of course, that we should be defeated upon them. Then we could go to the country with this illustration of what we would do if we had a Socialist majority. This was a course that had been urged by the extreme wing of the party, but

127

it was not a policy which commended itself to reasonable opinion. I urged very strongly to this meeting that we should not adopt an extreme policy but should confine our legislative proposals to measures that we were likely to be able to carry...We must show the country that we were not under the domination of the wild men.'[159] Compare this to the constant references to 'cautiousness' by Tony Blair in the run-up to the 1997 election. Also, 'New Labour', and therefore the five very limited election pledges of 1997, were the creation of a very small number of people, of whom Blair, Mandelson, Philip Gould and Alastair Campbell were the most important. The similarities are uncanny and yet not accidental. The two governments are directly connected by a commitment to labourism.

An absence of ideology

Turning to the characteristics of this phenomenon for the final time, the first to be examined will be that of the lack of a clear ideology. That this is necessarily a criticism cannot be assumed. Many politicians from different parties make a virtue of their pragmatism and suggest that ideology is both restricting and unnecessary and even an encumbrance. Tony Blair, in the introduction to Labour's 1997 election manifesto *New Labour, because Britain deserves better*, writes: 'We will be a radical government. But the definition of radicalism will not be that of doctrine, whether of left or right, but of achievement. New Labour is a party of ideas and ideals but not of outdated ideology. What counts is what works.'[160] Ian Gilmour (1977) in his study of Conservatism wrote: '...as philosophy or doctrine is concerned, the wise Conservative travels light. Conservative principles cannot be precisely tabulated.'[161]

However, when the dictionary definition of ideology is examined: '...the system of ideas at the basis of an economic or political theory...',[162] it seems sufficiently innocuous to raise the question of the desirability of ideology, particularly for a political party. Should a political party have a stated and clear ideology? If not, why not? One answer could be to enable it to appeal to a wider cross-section of the population, and for an electoral party such as Labour this would appear to have some legitimacy. However, in response one might ask the basis of this appeal: 'What does the party actually stand for? When I vote for Labour, what am I voting for?' The British Labour Party has always sought to answer these questions as vaguely as possible.

It is not just Tony Blair who specializes in rhetorical and ambiguous language. Labour leaders since MacDonald have shrouded the aims of the party in mystery. MacDonald thought that the policy of a 'socialistic party', as he referred to it, should be based: '...not on functions (like labour), but on the complete civic unity to which functions are only contributory, and upon the citizen, of whom the worker is only a differentiated and specialised aspect...The community idea must be the dominant note: the thought must be of the co-operation of citizens, not of workmen nor of consumers.'[163] There are many similarities between the language and vague sentiments of MacDonald in 1920, and those of Tony Blair in the late 1990s. In 1909 MacDonald wrote: '...Socialism is to come through a socialistic political party and not through a Socialist one. Indeed, paradoxical though it may appear, Socialism will be retarded by a Socialist party which thinks it can do better than a Socialistic party, because its methods would be contrary to those by which Society evolves.'[164] Compare this to Blair's statement: 'This is my socialism...It is not the socialism of Marx or state control. It is rooted in a straightforward view of society: in the understanding that the individual does best in a strong and decent community of people, with principles and standards and common aims and values. It is socialism.'[165] Both leaders are trying to provide personal, and somewhat superficial, revisions of socialist ideas. Note also the actual similarity of the content of their 'socialism'.

The one enduring value that Labour leaders have espoused throughout is that of the commitment to 'social justice'. To suggest that this is vague is axiomatic within the context of this book, but the vagueness of this concept surpasses that of most of the others employed. In the 1920s Philip Snowden wrote: '..the Labour Party is working for justice for all men and women of every class who live by honest and useful work.'[166] Clement Attlee's New Year message to the labour movement in 1951 contained the following: 'We are seeking to build a free democratic society based on social justice.'[167]

The 1955 party election manifesto concluded with the words: 'The powers that we ask for will be used in the interests of the whole nation, fully respecting the rights of human personality. Our aim is to make men more truly free. In 1945, Britain started out along the path of social justice. Now is the time to go forward with Labour.'[168] The revisionists of the late 1950s and early 1960s thought that: '...socialism was a philosophy of distributional justice whose main aims were greater equality, social justice and the preservation of full employment.'[169] Harold Wilson told the 1972 party conference: '...there can be no road to national agreement, national unity, on a policy adequate for dealing with inflation and unemployment except on the basis of social justice.'[170]

In 1992, John Smith, as the new leader of the Labour Party, created the Commission on Social Justice. This is how, in its final report, it defined social justice: 'First, a free society needs to be founded upon the equal worth of all citizens expressed in equality before the law, political and civil liberties...Second, all citizens are entitled to have their basic needs for food, income, shelter and health met by the state. Third, in order to ensure self respect and equal citizenship there must be the widest possible access to opportunities and life chances and fourth, to achieve the first three conditions it is important to recognise that not all inequalities are unjust, but that those that are should 'be reduced and where possible eliminated'.[171] This seems to be little more than a re-statement of 'Liberty, Equality and Fraternity' without the fraternity!

Unsurprisingly, Tony Blair adds to this historical litany of rhetorical commitments to social justice. He devotes a whole chapter to it in his book *New Britain, My Vision of a Young Country* (1996), which concludes: 'Social justice is not a matter of altruism. It is about self-interest and common interest. Social justice is about building a nation to be proud of. It is not devoted to levelling down, or taking from the successful and giving to the unsuccessful. It is about levelling up.'[172] The only thing that this appears to add to the numerous references to social justice made throughout the century is the influence of Thatcherism.

The notion of social justice is perhaps the one overriding principle that the party has committed itself to right throughout its history. However, it has mainly remained undefined and has always been interpreted as vaguely as possible. The clearest statement of the ideology of the newly-formed Labour Representation Committee is to be found in their first ever manifesto, for the general election of 1900. As already stated in chapter two, after listing a number of radical measures, this manifesto concludes: 'The object of these measures is to enable the people ultimately to obtain the Socialisation of the Means of Production, Distribution and Exchange, to be controlled by a Democratic State in the interests of the entire Community, and the Complete Emancipation of Labour from the Domination of Capitalism and Landlordism, with the Establishment of Social and Economic Equality between the Sexes.'[173] However, this clarity of overall purpose did not appear again in Labour literature or speeches. Ross McKibbin (1974), as noted in the second chapter, cites the origins of this lack of clarity of purpose in the 1900 conference which created the LRC: 'Effectively, the conference which met at the Memorial Hall, Faringdon Street, in February 1900, was agreed upon independent Labour representation, but upon little else. It was assumed that the new party would defend the 'interests' of the working class in parliament and protect the threatened privileges of the unions, but it had no other 'objective' other than the negative one that it renounced support for all other parties.'[174] In fact, even the latter was qualified in 1900 by: '...a readiness to co-operate with any party which for the time being may be engaged in promoting legislation in the direct interest of labour, and be equally ready to associate with any party in opposing measures having an opposite tendency.'[175]

This absence of a clear ideology has contributed enormously to the lack of success of the party, electorally and in more general terms. In fact, it can be shown that the party has achieved the most success when it has presented, to the electorate, the clearest possible message as regards its intentions when in government. While these statements did not have a clear ideological basis, they nevertheless communicated relatively clearly to the electorate what the party intended to do, once it was in government. Thus in 1945, the Labour Party offered full employment, public ownership of basic industries, a house-building programme and a National Health Service. In 1966, Harold Wilson offered a National Plan, a house-building programme, a programme of urban renewal, full employment and a modernization of parliament, and in 1997 Tony Blair offered the five key election pledges. These rare moments of comparative clarity were the products of either particular historical conjunctures such as the end of the Second World War and the defeat of fascism, or the emergence of a strong leader such as Tony Blair, or both, as in the case of Harold Wilson and the 'spirit of the 1960s'. During the intervening periods, for a great deal of the time, Labour procrastinated or was beset with internal disputes precisely because it did not have a clear ideology from its inception. As Mr H. Quelch of the SDF put it at the first annual conference of the LRC in 1901: 'The movement could be too broad. It must have a basis before it had breadth.'[176] Needless to say, Mr Quelch's admonishments went unheeded.

A confused and confusing policy-making process

This lack of an ideological basis, then, has had a concomitant effect on the elements of a political party that would be built upon this foundation. The lack of a clearly stated set of principles, which is all an ideology ultimately is, means that policy-making necessarily and inevitably becomes a somewhat confused, piecemeal and reactive process. If the history of Labour Party policy-making is examined, it can be shown that this is the case.

In fact, even the resolution at the 1900 foundation conference, moved by Keir Hardie, which gave the new organisation its aims and commitments was an amendment to the 'class war' resolution of the Social Democratic Federation. A Mr James MacDonald of the SDF had moved the substantive resolution: 'That the representatives of the working-class movement in the House of Commons shall form there a distinct party, with a party organisation separate from the capitalist parties based upon a recognition of the class war, and having for its ultimate object, the socialisation of the means of production, distribution and exchange.'[177] Even at its inception, the aims of the party were defined as a negative response to an explicit statement of ideology and aims. This is an extremely important point.

Lewis Minkin (1978), in examining the period before 1918, draws attention to: '...the deep dissatisfaction with the performance of 'the parliamentary arm'. Between 1900 and 1914, the Conferences were small, assertive and often recriminatory.'[178] The independence of the MPs and particularly the leadership, then and now, has at least something to do with a lack of a clear ideology and stated aims. The absence of the latter allows the development of autonomy of representation because there is no consensus on what the party stands for. Minkin refers to it as 'parliamentary elitism'.

In 1918, the party adopted a new constitution of local parties and individual membership. Trade unions and socialist societies could affiliate at local as well as national level and the party conference was comprised of delegates from nationally affiliated organisations and local constituency parties. The unions continued to dominate at both levels and the composition of the new NEC reflected this dominance, with thirteen out of twenty-three seats being allotted to the unions. In theory it was '...the duty of every Parliamentary representative of the Party to be guided by the decision of the meetings of such Parliamentary representatives, with a view to giving effect to the decisions of the Party Conference...'[179] but in practice this was hardly ever the case. Policy formulation, from 1918 right through to the constitutional changes of 1997, was a somewhat confused process involving sometimes tenuous and strained relationships between the party conference, the NEC, the parliamentary party and last, but certainly not least, the party leadership. In theory, the process was a relatively straightforward and democratic one. In practice it was confused, piecemeal and involved a great many 'personality clashes'. Perhaps there is an inevitability as regards the latter: people will always be in conflict when power is at stake. However, the level of this conflict in the Labour Party could have been much reduced, and the nature of it changed, if the individuals concerned knew what they were ultimately arguing for and about. That is, if there were agreed aims and objectives for the party from the outset, or at any other time in its history.

Thus Hugh Gaitskell, the party leader, was able to respond to the decision to support unilateral nuclear disarmament at the 1960 conference, without any reference to a substantive argument, by saying: 'What sort of people do you think we are? Do you think we can simply accept a decision of this kind?'[180]

The conflict between the party and the leadership over policy manifested itself immediately after the creation of the new constitution in 1918. A special party conference decided to terminate membership of the coalition government of the time. Many of the Labour ministers strongly opposed the decision and fought the subsequent election as independent candidates. Of the situation between 1918 and 1922, Minkin writes: 'At the Party Conference the performance of Labour M.P.'s was subject to persistent criticism, and the decisions taken were not always to the liking of the P.L.P. On the N.E.C., policy initiation continued with little consultation of the parliamentary group, a fact which caused a great deal of resentment, especially over the influential role played by extra-parliamentary figures like Henderson and Sidney Webb.'[181]

These conflicts, and the confusion surrounding them, have been ably documented by Minkin in two excellent books; one on the party conference (1978) and the other on the relationship between the trade unions and the party (1991). It is noteworthy that in both books Minkin relates these conflicts to the whole of the party's history.

Instead of possessing an ideology which would, at the very least, provide guidance for policy-making, Labour's pragmatism means that it adopts policies and positions that reflect the prevailing ideas and even fashions of a particular time. For example, it was anti-imperialist and pro home rule in the early part of the century, for Keynesian intervention, welfare and full employment after the Second World War, unilateralist and 'modern' in the 1960s, corporatist in the 1970s and neo-monetarist and 'new' in the 1990s.

In 1997 the party made a huge change to the way in which it makes policy. This will be examined in some detail later in the chapter but it should be noted here that the new procedures add neither clarity nor purpose to the decision-making process and, in fact, highly complicate it to the extent of making it almost totally incomprehensible.

'Pragmatism' over principles

Both a lack of ideology and a confused approach to policy-making contribute to the vagueness of purpose that was outlined in the first chapter of this book. This has inevitably led to the party almost always emphasizing the importance of 'pragmatism over principles'. It is this notion that allowed the Labour Party, and movement, to adopt Keynesian economic ideas and Beveridge's 'welfarism' during the Second World War. These ideas were by no means social democratic in origin and yet they formed the economic and political basis of labourism, and indeed conservatism, in Britain for approximately thirty-five of the post-war years. In fact they did the same for most of the major political parties throughout the Western industrialised nations.

Keynesianism within labourism has now been replaced by a neo-liberal, monetarist-inspired approach to economic policy. That this is the case as regards the current Labour Government is shown by Gordon Brown's constant repetition of the words 'sound public finances' and 'prudence'.

It is this willingness to 'change with the times' that Tony Blair referred to in his speech to the Fabian Society in 1995 on the 50th anniversary of the 1945 general election: '…it is important to understand where that government's strength came from, what it really represented as well as what it did not. The reality…is that the Labour Government's agenda grew out of the coalition government of the war; that *it cut decisively with not against the grain of political thinking* [my italics]; and that its prospectus at the election was strongest in the new direction it offered, not the minutiae of policy detail.'[182] and: 'Our values do not change. Our commitment to a different vision of society stands intact. But the ways of achieving that vision must change. The programme we are in the process of constructing entirely reflects our values. Its objectives would be instantly recognisable to our founders... What have changed are the means of achieving these objectives'.[183]

Accordingly, neo-liberal economic policy replaces Keynesianism, despite their completely different emphases and effects as regards the key issue of 'social justice', and the welfare state is under attack as regards the principles of 'universality' and 'need'. Instead vague notions of 'targeting' the poorest are expounded along with insistence upon private provision for such things as pensions. However, the government, so far, has found it very difficult to reform the welfare state. Indeed, the then Secretary of State, Harriet Harman, lost her job in the Cabinet re-shuffle of July 1998, and Frank Field, the Minister for Welfare Reform, resigned as a result. This represents Blair attempting to 'cut with the grain of political thinking' of the current monetarist orthodoxy and, in the case of 'welfare reform', failing spectacularly to implement it in practice.

The lack of an ideology allows Blair, as previous leaders before him, to adopt the prevailing economic ideology with, apparently, very few contradictions for him and the party to deal with. However, the difficulties with welfare reform, the simmering discontent of Labour backbenchers and members, the support for left-wingers in the elections to the NEC in 1998 and 1999, the fox-hunting debate, the debacle over the leadership of the Welsh Parliament, divisions over reform of the House of Lords, the conflicts over state pensions at the 2000 conference, and, not least, the circus of the selection of the London Mayoral candidate, plus many other issues, are all manifestations of the contradictions inherent within labourism, which are the products of an absence of a clear, stated ideology. To represent labour without any clear notion of the nature and content of that representation, in an economic system that favours the interests of capital, necessarily involves the leadership in constant contortions and 'deal-doings' which are then given the respectable label of 'pragmatism'.

An absence of ideology or even clear aims inevitably, therefore, involves the Labour Party in a confused policy formulation process which always emphasises the importance of pragmatism over any principles. In fact, given that the latter have never existed in a coherent sense for the whole party and movement, the leadership is left with arguing for this vacuous and ultimately meaningless notion of pragmatism. Pragmatism must have a basis from which to proceed: all human practical activity is informed by theory, even if in a very oblique and indirect way. Thus, to attempt to create a political party without an agreed ideology or even a set of principles is merely attempting to create 'form without content'. This certainly does not correspond with Bernstein's notion of evolutionary socialism, nor with very much West European social democratic thinking on the subject. As we saw in Chapter One, both Nairn and Desai attribute the causes of this notion of 'pragmatism' to a profound anti-intellectualism in the labour movement in the late nineteenth century and throughout its history. While this is no doubt the case, merely asserting that the labour movement was and is anti-intellectual fails to explain why. British society itself is generally anti-intellectual: perhaps this is one of the factors contributing to its acceptance as the *raison-d'etre* of the party?

These first three characteristics can be summarised under the general heading of 'vagueness of purpose'. It has never been clear exactly, or even imprecisely, what the Labour Party stands for at any time throughout its history. Instead, aims and objectives have been largely obscured by rhetoric and vagueness. Ralph Miliband (1972) should be acknowledged here as the original source and inspiration for these three characteristics of labourism. However, it is also very appropriate to quote R.H. Tawney from 1931: 'The great weakness of British Labour…is its lack of a creed. The Labour Party is hesitant in action because divided in mind. It does not achieve what it could because it does not know what it wants.'[184]

The Labour Party – national or 'sectional'?

The next characteristic to be examined will be that of the party always presenting itself as representing the national or general interest when, in fact, it emerged from a very clearly delineated section of the population – trade unions and other 'working-class' interest groups. This contradiction cannot be overemphasized. The Labour Representation Committee was created by the trade unions and the much smaller socialist societies. The influence on the party of 'trade-union ideology', in the broadest possible sense, has been examined in Chapters One and Two, as has the influence of the ILP's socialism, the

SDF's revolutionary socialism and the Fabian Society's gradualism. It is only the latter that has had enduring influence, while the ILP's 'means over ends' approach to politics in the closing stages of the nineteenth century has been incorporated into the *raison d'être* of labourism. In fact, labourism could not have come into being without this vital input from the ILP – the notion that parliamentary representation of working people was more important than the specification of the content of that representation. Apart from this, though, the ideas, policies and approach of the ILP have largely disappeared from the armoury of labourism. They are kept alive by only a very small element of the Labour Left.

Importantly, however, it was from trade union and, to a much lesser extent socialist, origins that the party came and it has never ceased to be, in a sense, a trade-union party. In 1918, when the new party constitution was introduced, the unions still continued to dominate the decision-making procedures of the party, including at local level, at the party conference and on the NEC. Thirteen out of twenty-three places on this newly constituted NEC were reserved for the unions. Minkin (1978) writes of 1918: 'Though in formal terms...the Party was seen to move away from its role as a trade union pressure group, the unions still retained a considerable potential for control.'[185]

The range of analogies that have been used to describe the trade union-party relationship is colourful, from Ernest Bevin's 'out of the bowels of the trade unions', through 'a ball and chain' and a pair of scissors metaphors to likening the relationship to a family: '...symbiotic, intense, at times tragic, but essentially indissoluble.'[186] Minkin (1991) traces the threats of separation of the party from the unions back to 1931. However, he ultimately asserts the strong and permanent character of the relationship.

The main elements of the symbiotic nature of the relationship are the financial support of the party by the unions and, in turn, the voting rights for the unions at party conference, on the NEC and elsewhere. While in recent decades the party has sought to play down the extent of these two key elements, primarily to placate the media, their significance and strength should not be underemphasized. Even as late as 1990 the trade unions commanded 5,347,000 votes out of an estimated total of 6,038,000 at the party conference.[187] This represents trade union control of approximately 88 per cent of the voting rights! However, in

1993 the weight of the union's block vote at conference was reduced to 70 per cent and this was further reduced in 1996 to 50 per cent. This remains the proportion of union voting rights at conference under the *Partnership in Power* proposals adopted in 1997. Also, the unions have retained the procedure of block voting under these new arrangements. Despite the general reduction in trade union influence in decision-making within the party, the new constitutional arrangements under *Partnership in Power* give the unions twelve out of a total of thirty-two representatives on the NEC and thirty out of a total of 175 representatives on the National Policy Forum.

While the party has been characterized by some commentators, throughout its history, as the political instrument of trade unionism, this is clearly not the case. If labourism was merely 'the politics of trade-unionism' as described by Hodgskin in the early nineteenth century (see Chapter One), there would be little need for any in-depth analysis of its nature. It would merely be striving to better the lot of wage-earners by parliamentary and local government means. Unfortunately, labourism in the twentieth century has come to mean something much more convoluted and complex than this. Importantly, despite this it was from a trade-union base that the party was created and an 'ideology', if that term can be used to describe something so vague, was imparted. This particularly manifested itself in limited aims, a cautious approach and a willingness to compromise, all of which came from the nature of the collective bargaining procedure which is the fundamental element of trade unionism.

Trade union funding of Labour has taken a number of forms. There are the direct contributions made by unions, both in the form of affiliation fees and one-off payments, during election campaigns, for example. There was also, until February 1996, the sponsorship of individual MPs by particular trade unions. Blair saw these as too much of a liability as regards the media and persuaded the unions to fund local party organisations in marginal seats instead. In 1991 there were over sixty trade unions nationally affiliated to the Labour Party, each paying substantial sums, plus a number of other unions not affiliated but with political funds with which they supported the party. In 1968 the trade unions provided 80 per cent of the Labour Party's income.[188] By 1995 this had fallen to 54 per cent of a total income of £12.5 million.[189] By 1998 this had decreased further to approximately 30 per cent of a total of £21 million. However, the unions provided a total of £9.6 million towards the cost of the 1997 election campaign.[190]

So even in the year 2001, when the distance between the party and the unions is the greatest it has ever been, the unions still retain a relatively high degree of influence in the Labour Party. While Tony Blair makes a show, for the media, of shunning the unions by insisting that they are on an equal footing with the CBI, as regards access to the government, Gordon Brown often welcomes union delegations and generally has cordial relations with them. Trade union representatives sit on a number of key government committees including an advisory committee on joining the single European currency and the New Deal Task Force. So it is with some legitimacy that the Labour Party can currently be described as, if not a 'trade-union party', one which still has very close links with the unions.

In 1903, in an article in the *New Liberal Review*, Ramsay MacDonald wrote: 'If the new Labour movement were simply an attempt of Trade Unionists to use their political power for purely sectional ends…it would be a menace to all the qualities that mark public life with distinction and honour…Trade Unionism in politics must identify itself with something higher and wider than Trade Union industrial demands. It must set those demands into a system of national well-being; the wage-earner must become the citizen; the union must become the guardian of economic justice.'[191] In the 1945 general election campaign, Clement Attlee stated: 'Forty years ago the Labour Party might with some justice have been called a class Party, representing almost exclusively the wage earners. It is still based on organised labour but has steadily become more and more inclusive…The Labour Party is, in fact, the one Party which most nearly reflects in its representation and composition all the main streams which flow into the great river of our national life…Our appeal to you, therefore, is not narrow or sectional…We have to plan the broad lines of our national life so that all may have the duty and the opportunity of rendering service to the nation, everyone in his or her sphere, and that all may help to create and share in an increasing material prosperity free from the fear of want.'[192]

Harold Wilson's famous 'white heat' speech to the Labour conference of 1963 also appealed to 'national' rather than 'sectional' interest. Part of it ran: '…we are re-stating our Socialism in terms of the scientific revolution…The Britain that is going to be forged in the white heat of this revolution will be no place for restrictive practices or out-dated methods on either side of industry.'[193] Tony Blair, equally and very vociferously, claims to represent the nation rather than a sectional interest; 'I ask in the name of this country's future – forget the past, no more bosses versus workers – we are on the same side, the same team, and Britain united will win!'[194] and: 'We are a national party, supported today by people from all walks of life, from the successful businessman or woman to the pensioner on a council estate...New Labour is the political arm of none other than the British people as a whole.'[195]

The repetition of the slogan 'New Britain' and its sentiments by both the Wilson and Blair modernizers is noteworthy, as we have seen in Chapter Two. Labour leaders and others, from MacDonald to Blair, have been very keen to emphasize the national interest over a sectional one. This is directly linked to their electoralist concerns. The electoralist dilemma of the party is admirably expressed by David Marquand (1992): 'The Labour Party has faced essentially the same problem since the 1920s: how to transcend Labourism without betraying the labour interest; how to bridge the gap between the old Labour fortresses and the potentially anti-Conservative, but non-Labour hinterland; how to construct a broad-based and enduring social coalition capable, not just of giving it a temporary majority in the House of Commons, but of sustaining a reforming government thereafter.'[196] Blair indicated his concurrence with this argument by quoting it in his 1995 speech to the Fabian Society celebrating the 50th anniversary of the 1945 government.

Labour's electoralism is a subject that has been much commented upon in the literature and was referred to in the first chapter. It is some-thing that pervades all of the characteristics described here. Essentially it is a concern with being 'electable' at almost any cost to its principles, scant as they are. Pandering to the requirements of the mass media has been the main form that this electoralism has taken in the 1990s. Presenting the party as a national rather than sectional one is the over-riding concern and this has always been the case. This concern with electoralism will be taken up again at the end of this chapter.

Women and the unemployed are two groups of people who have suffered a great deal as a result of labourism's exclusive concentration upon representing labour. The Suffragettes fought long and hard to establish universal female suffrage but the Labour Party, despite making claims in 1918 to be: '...The Real Women's Party...',[197] virtually ignored the needs of women unless they also happened to be wage-earners, right throughout the century. Likewise, the unemployed, apart from being provided with a welfare 'safety net' after the Second World War, have never really influenced the party's political agenda.

This attempt to appear 'national' while emerging from and, to a large extent, continuing with a clear 'sectional' interest – that of trade unions, working people and, to a much lesser extent, socialists – is a massive contradiction and one which constantly makes problems for the Labour leadership. The media, if they choose to, are able to refer to this aspect of labourism as a means of exposing any particular leader's claims to represent the nation. Even the name 'Labour' suggests the dominance of a particular interest group over all others.

Labour's emotional appeal

The next characteristic to be examined will be that of the party's and movement's capacity and willingness to appeal to the electorate, its membership, its MPs and even sections of its leadership in an emotional rather than a rational sense. Numerous examples of this can be found throughout history. Keir Hardie, in 1907, described socialism in the following way: '…the ugliness and squalor which now meets you at every turn in some of the most beautiful valleys in the world would disappear, the rivers would run pure and clear as they did of yore…and in the winter the log would glow on the fire the while that the youths and maidens made glad the heart with mirth and song, and there would be beauty and joy everywhere.'[198]

There was a large amount of rhetorical appeal to the emotions in Harold Wilson's 'white heat' speech of 1963, an example of which is: 'The problem is this…It is the choice between the blind imposition of technological advance, with all that means in terms of unemployment, and the conscious, planned, purposive use of scientific progress to provide undreamed of living standards and the possibility of leisure ultimately on an unbelievable scale…'[199]

While David Marquand (1992) writes of Kinnock's speaking skills: 'The myths and symbols of Labourism, which he manipulates with such artistry, are his myths and symbols: that is why the artistry is so successful.',[200] not everyone agrees. Heffernan and Marquesee (1992) write: 'Kinnock's notoriously prolix oratory reflected this combination of insecurity and arrogance. The confusing welter of clauses and subclauses, the pointless litanies and profuse alliteration were all an attempt to disguise a hollow core in an elaborate container.'[201] This latter metaphor could very well be used to describe the notion of labourism advanced in this book!

Tony Blair is a speaker who brings new meaning to rhetoric and appealing to the emotions. His conference speeches are good examples. The 1996 speech included the following, which mirrored Wilson's of 1963: 'As a father, as a leader, as a member of the human family, I ask this question of Britain's future. We live in an era of extraordinary, revolutionary change at work, at home, through technology, through the million marvels of modern science. The possibilities are exciting. But the challenge is clear. How do we create in Britain a new age of achievement in which all of the people – not just a few but all of the people – can share?'[202]

This emotional appeal is also particularly applicable in communities such as Sheffield, as is illustrated in the case study. In such communities it sometimes appears that the emotional appeal of labourism outweighs any other considerations as regards electoral and general support. 'I vote Labour because my father did and his father before him' is a particularly traditional example of this and even in the early twenty-first century this type of attitude can still be found. The general emotional appeal of Labour ranges over a great deal of its activities, from posters and other forms of propaganda, particularly in the early part of the century and the post-war period, through utterances of various kinds from party leaders, as shown above, to the creation of the Millennium Dome in Greenwich and 'Cool Britannia'. Apart from purely careerist considerations, an 'Old Labour' trade unionist such as John Prescott must have been persuaded to support New Labour on emotional as well as rational grounds.

The very fact that David Blunkett can transform himself from a radical 'anti-paternalist' socialist in the late 1970s and early 1980s to an authoritarian Secretary of State in the late 1990s, all within the boundaries of labourism, requires a suspension of rationality that can only be described as 'emotional' in nature. Labour voters who supported Blunkett then and support him now are being asked to stretch their loyalty to Labour to the utmost extremes. This process relies directly upon a vague emotional commitment to Labour and almost everything that it stands for, despite the difficulties in actually defining the latter in any rational manner. From Keynesian full employment to neo-liberal economic 'prudence' requires an equal stretching of loyalty through emotional rather than rational commitment. When Tony Blair warned the four new left-wing members of the National Executive Committee, at the beginning of the 1998 party conference, that their choice is not between the Labour Party of their dreams and the current Labour government, but between the Labour government and a Tory government, the question arose in one's mind: 'but is this actually a choice?' Perhaps the choice between New Labour and the Tories is more symbolic than real, and therefore emotional rather than rational.

To achieve power Labour is actually highly dependent upon its emotional appeal to the electorate as the party of 'social justice' and to members and trade unionists as part of 'the great movement'. This is as true of New Labour as it was of the party during any time in its existence. Frank Dobson's appearance as a slightly eccentric kindly old uncle and John Prescott's image of cloth-capped trade unionist are as useful to Blair in manipulating a politically somewhat ignorant electorate as their respective roles vis-à-vis health and deputy leadership and transport. Likewise his and Gordon Brown's images as educated, able and technocratic inspire respect and even awe in some sections of the electorate.

However, it is in a very general sense that Labour's emotional appeal is most successful. In some sections of 'traditional' Labour areas of the country, it would be perceived as almost heresy to vote for a party other than Labour and expressions approximating to 'you could put up a monkey in a red jacket and it would get elected' can be heard from Glasgow through Sheffield to parts of the East End of London. This traditional allegiance is both enduring and somewhat mysterious. Labour is perceived as fighting for the rights of working people and yet constantly, throughout its history, it has failed to do so. Despite these failures, the idea persists that the Labour Party will and does 'stand up for working-people', 'the working class', the 'working man' or 'the underdog'. Thus many Labour voters believed that there was at least an element of a 'Trojan Horse' strategy to Blair's election success in 1997. That is, he and other Labour leaders presented themselves as moderate and respectable to get elected, and then, once in power, would embark upon radical and perhaps even some 'socialist' political actions. In fact, nothing could be further from the truth. New Labour's 1997 manifesto was not a smokescreen hiding left radicalism. If anything, the 'social' commitments regarding NHS waiting lists and school classroom sizes for five, six and seven year-olds attempted to conceal the extent to which the party had moved to the right.

Labour's success in the 1997 and previous elections was directly dependent upon a vague emotional appeal to the electorate on the issue of 'social justice'. Blair's constant imploring of the electorate to trust him was as disingenuous as it was excruciating. The nature of this appeal can be compared to that of the Tory appeal to patriotism, national pride and 'family values'. This is equally emotional in nature, often to conceal the absence of specific policies that are able to deliver on these things.

Labour's emotional appeal is vast, somewhat amorphous and is often transmitted through the generations. It is absolutely essential in gaining and keeping both general and electoral support. It operates at both the level of the individual and the collective. It is therefore one of the key characteristics of labourism. One of the ways that this has manifested itself in the 1990s is the manipulation of information so as to make it acceptable to the mass media, the so-called 'spin-doctoring' so efficiently managed by Mandelson and Campbell. This is emotional rather than rational in nature in that it often panders to the worst prejudices of sections of the British population. Thus Jack Straw was able to criticize 'squeegee merchants' and beggars in the run-up to the general election campaign of 1997. Likewise, controversial issues such as sexual orientation are kept off the media agenda until they are rudely forced on to it by such things as Ron Davies taking a walk on Clapham Common. The presentation of information via the media is as stage-managed as the Labour Party Conference. A positive gloss is put upon virtually every aspect of the government's activities. However, what is referred to here as positive largely relates to traditional and conventional family-orien-tated values. Homosexuality, single-parenthood, alternative lifestyles and many other things are either ignored, confined to the periphery of polit-ical concern or even criticized. Thus the stereotype of deviancy is reinforced. Jack Straw, as Home Secretary, apparently thought it completely acceptable to voice his 'personal opinion' of opposition to adoption by lesbians and gay men and lesbian IVF mothers in November 1997. Likewise with the concentration on, and scapegoating of, single parents and asylum seekers. All these reinforce the ignorance and preju-dices of sections of the population and are, thus, emotional in nature.

There is nothing wrong per se with appealing to a person's emotions along with their intellect. Even members and supporters of political parties have emotions and it is not being argued here that political activity precludes emotional life. On the contrary, emotions are as important in politics as they are in any other aspect of human social life. However, it is being argued that the type of emotional appeal that labourism employs is vague, vacuous and ultimately misleading and manipulative. Appeals based on the vague notions of 'the march forward', 'the great movement', 'social justice' and even 'inevitable gradualism' suggest that there is a long-term aim or even an 'end' to Labour's politics. This is simply untrue. The vagaries of Labour's electoralist politics guarantee that this end, this goal, even if it was ever defined, will never be reached. Labour supporters will always be either aiming, striving, fighting or, much more often, waiting for something that doesn't actually exist, even in theory. The emotional appeal that successive leaderships and party members have employed to gain support is cynical, manipulative and simply unacceptable.

Labour never has been, and is not, a genuine social democratic party in the sense that the Swedish party, for example, was. Thus it has always, in a very subtle manner, been involved in an element of deception of its electorate. It has had to convince them that it has the capacity to represent them without actually having it, so emotional appeals to 'solidarity', 'social justice', the 'great movement' etc. have been necessary electoral tools. The very absence of ideology and the vagueness of purpose have required this to be the case. As McKibbin (1974) stated of the inclusion of Clause Four in the party's constitution in 1918: 'A Party with a socialist objective but no socialist ideology needs something else: the movement and service to the movement became a substitute.'[203] It has always appealed to its electorate, its membership and its supporters in an emotional manner and has lacked the capacity to actually represent their interests. It is in this sense, then, that this emotional appeal is disingenuous.

The lack of democracy and excessive bureaucracy

The Labour Party and movement are undemocratic and bureaucratic. This statement obviously needs some justification. Since 1918 Labour has presented itself as the most internally democratic party in Britain. It has prided itself on its democratic structures, its policy-making forums, its elections for office (low and high) and its general culture of democratic debate and decision-making. In fact, this is the one area in which

the party has changed substantially in the last two years and it will therefore be examined in some detail.

As early as 1907, Keir Hardie, the first leader of the Labour Party,
announced that: '…he would resign rather than obey a Conference
instruction on Female Suffrage if it should run counter to his own
views.'[204] He made it quite clear that he opposed instruction by
anybody, including conference. Successive party leaders have adopted
this attitude and carried it out in practice, and at the same time argued
that the Labour Party is the most internally democratic political party in
Britain!

The Labour Party is, in fact, the most internally democratic political
party in Britain *in theory*. Its extensive constitutional structures and
procedures, the bases of which were put in place in 1918, create the
potential for a thoroughgoing and accountable form of democracy. The
problematic relationship between the Party Conference, the NEC and
the Parliamentary Party, particularly its leadership, has been referred to
earlier in the chapter. However, the new constitution of 1918 gave 'sovereignty' to the party conference: 'The object of the Party was 'to give effect
as far as may be practicable to the principles from time to time approved
by the Party Conference'…'[205] While the language of this statement
cannot exactly be described as unequivocal, nevertheless it is clear that
the conference was intended to be the sovereign body of the party and
this continued to be the case right up until 1997. In fact, the authors of
the document that brought the constitutional changes of that year into
effect also claim that 'Annual conference remains the sovereign policy
and decision-making body of the Labour Party.'[206] While the latter statement is strongly disagreed with here, it is included to reiterate the
importance of the notion of the conference as sovereign body. This idea
has underpinned the belief in the democracy of the party.

However, in practice successive leaderships have cynically manipulated these structures and procedures to obtain the result that they want
and, if defeated, have either ignored the democratic decisions or, at best,
paid lip-service to them. Minkin (1978) states it in a more subtle
manner: 'In the Party's policy-making process, and in the degree to
which they could tactically use the areas of discretion constitutionally
open to them, the leaders of the P.L.P. became the most important
policy-making group in the Party, at least for much of its history.'[207] A
substantial part of the problem is to do with the fact that the party

started life as a parliamentary representation committee and then tried to extend itself from the top-down. The fact that the party did not start from the grassroots, building upwards to create a national party, is a very important aspect of the undemocratic nature of the party.

During the period from 1918, when the Labour Party's constitution and structure were created, to 1997, when the new policy-making structures under *Partnership in Power* were put into place, the Labour Party did have, in theory, the most internally democratic regime of all of the major political parties in Britain. However, in practice, right throughout its history, the leadership of the party continually and consistently ignored many of the party's policies. Many of these leaders habitually and systematically ignored decisions made at conference and displayed an arrogant dismissiveness and total lack of consideration for the party's democracy. McKenzie (1963) recognizes this in his classic study of British political parties. After citing Attlee plus a document issued by party head office, both on the sovereignty of the annual conference, he writes: 'These passages grossly exaggerate the role of the conference in the affairs of the Labour Party. They appear to imply that Labour MPs and hence, by implication, the PLP and even a Labour Government must be subject to the direction of the annual conference; but...the PLP is autonomous and the annual conference has no control whatsoever over the actions of a Labour Government.'[208]

Even if theoretically democratic, many of the procedures employed and structures created were and are overly bureaucratic. For a new member joining the party its decision-making process seem to involve a maze of committees and other bodies, the existence of which seem to be justified with reference to the democracy of the party but which generally serve to obscure undemocratic and secretive practices. Any member or trade union representative wishing to question a decision is faced with the issue of rules and procedure and can often be silenced by a reference to a technicality of which he or she had little knowledge. This bureaucratic aspect of labour movement decision-making is very well known and is perceived as either an essential protection of democracy or an unnecessary encumbrance which can be manipulated in an undemocratic manner. The reality is that in practice the structures and procedures of the Labour Party, and movement, that were created to enhance democracy, have generally been used, throughout its history, in a manipulative and undemocratic way.

As regards the notion of the conference being the sovereign body of the party, the process of replacing it with the idea of being the showcase for the leadership began in earnest in 1985 with the appointment, by Kinnock, of Peter Mandelson as Director of Campaigns and Communication. It was from that year that the conference became progressively more stage-managed. Two things, as regards this stage-management, happened in 1997. The constitutional changes of that year merely institutionalized and made formal the leadership practices that had been occurring since 1918. Up until then the leadership had acted in such a manner as to wilfully ignore the democratic wishes of the party membership. The constitutional changes of *Partnership in Power* formally and institutionally sanctions these undemocratic practices. Also, the process of managing the conference to avoid unseemly rows and open conflicts upon which the media could capitalize was finally concluded. The acceptance of the proposals on constitutional change in *Partnership in Power*, represented the victory of Mandelson's news management campaign, which he had been fighting since 1985.

Thus, in 1998 it had apparently become acceptable for Diana Jeuda, a member of Labour's NEC, to say: 'Where the government is wrong, I will continue to argue about that. I will be saying it privately to Tony. I don't think its good. I will not be saying that to the press in any big way...'[209] 'Smoke-filled rooms' style decision-making has now become formally institutionalised within the party and therefore can apparently be talked about openly.

The proposals contained in *Partnership in Power* involved the creation of a number of new bodies including a Joint Policy Committee, Standing Commissions and Regional and Local Policy Forums and the National Policy Forum. The process involves a very complicated inter-action between these and community groups, voluntary agencies, individuals, trade unions and constituency Labour parties – a process too complex to explain here and certainly one too complicated for the average Labour Party member to immediately grasp. The rationale provided for introducing these changes was as follows: '...Party Conference is a showpiece: of our policies and ways of establishing them, for our members and affiliates, for our voters and supporters in the country, for the press and media and for other political parties and those who support them. When Labour is in power, Party Conference also becomes a main showcase for the Prime Minister, other members of the

Government and for a review of progress and achievements...The more controversial or significant the debates and other events at Party Conference, the more they attract sensational press attention. Gladiatorial contests and deeply divisive conflicts particularly capture attention, irrespective of their true significance; and the alleged power and influence of key individuals, unions or groups are emphasised. As far as possible, and without detracting from the democratic decision making powers of the Conference, we need to beware of providing opportunities for external opponents and critics of the Party to pinpoint Conference as an example of difficulties for the Party in power.'[210]

So, it appears that the main reasons for changing the policy-making process were presentational in nature rather than substantial. These proposals were passed at the 1997 party conference. As compared to the 'old' method of making policy, they are even more complicated, unwieldy and almost completely inaccessible.

As regards the internal democratic structures of the party, then, much changed in 1997. The party conference went from being the sovereign policy-making body to being a 'show-case' for the party leadership. As already noted, this process had started a number of years earlier but it was only formalized with the adoption of *Partnership in Power* by the 1997 party conference. Until 1997 the leadership largely ignored the democratically-expressed wishes of the party membership. After 1997, the new formal democratic structures of the party gave such power to the leadership that it no longer needed to. Furthermore, *Partnership in Power* dramatically increases the bureaucracy of party decision-making. The complexity of these new structures is almost beyond belief. The idea that they simplify or streamline decision-making processes, as is claimed, is incredible.

The 'culture of defeatism'

The final characteristic of labourism that will be examined is that of 'the culture of defeatism' within the party and movement, again right throughout its history. This concept needs some explanation. It is a very broad-ranging idea that, essentially, the Labour Party and movement concedes defeat before the fight has even begun. This is conceived of here in a social democratic context. That is, the criticism being made is not that the party and movement avoids socialist policies and practices. Rather it is that the party and movement does not put even social democratic ideas into practice. Likewise, it has avoided being a movement for educational and hegemonic change. As we have seen, it has passively accepted the prejudices and ignorance of sections of the electorate rather than even attempting to change them. The reasons for this are somewhat complicated and are inter-connected with many other issues. Fear of failure is one explanation. The limited and vague aims of labourism are obviously another. If a party does not actually know what it stands for, how can it put *any* ideas into practice effectively? A notion of the reserved nature of the British character might inform the political, and specifically electoral, timidity of labourism. Individual and collective psychology appear to play a part but this is perhaps not the place to pursue this particular issue.

Numerous examples of this phenomenon can be found throughout Labour's history. Just three months after the LRC had been formed, it decided to approach the other two parties regarding the possibility of electoral pacts and in 1903, after secret negotiations between MacDonald, Hardie and Herbert Gladstone, the Liberal Chief Whip, such a pact was formed, although this was denied by both Hardie and MacDonald. Given that the aim of the LRC was independent representation of labour, it does seem somewhat defeatist to immediately go into negotiations with the Liberals regarding electoral arrangements. This timidity can also be seen in the very limited ambitions of the first ever Labour government of 1924 referred to earlier in the chapter.

The resolution of the 1926 General Strike is an obvious example of Labour's timidity. Miliband (1972) writes: 'The calling off of the General Strike without any guarantee of any kind, either for the miners or against the victimization of other workers, has often been denounced as a terrible act of betrayal. But the notion of betrayal, though accurate, should not be allowed to reduce the episode to the scale of a Victorian melodrama, with the Labour leaders as the gleeful villains, planning and perpetrating an evil deed. The Labour movement was betrayed, but not because the Labour leaders were villains, or cowards. It was betrayed because betrayal was the inherent and inescapable consequence of their whole philosophy of politics...'[211] This book concurs completely with this characterization of Labour leadership's tendencies to unilaterally declare surrender. In practice 'betrayal' was the operation, of a vague, unprincipled and undemocratic approach to the issue of political strategy.

In 1951, after six years of radical, reforming activity, it appears that the Labour Party simply ran out of ideas! Miliband refers to the period as 'the climax of Labourism'. The election manifesto of 1951, as compared with those of 1945 and 1950, is notably devoid of detail and much more rhetorical. Thus a party whose whole *raison d'être* for more than half a century had been to try to gain an overall majority in the House of Commons appears to have simply given up the fight, with the attitude of letting the Conservatives 'have their turn' at government! This is a particularly depressing example of this 'culture of defeatism'.

The fiasco around Peter Tatchell's selection as Labour's prospective parliamentary candidate for the constituency of Bermondsey in South London, which began in 1981, is a tremendous example of the party leadership 'shooting itself in the foot'. Initially Michael Foot, as party leader, publicly declared that Tatchell, because of statements he had made regarding the desirability of 'extra-parliamentary action', would not receive official endorsement as a candidate. After going through many and varied stages, including Tatchell being banned as a candidate and subsequently re-instated and reconciled with Foot, all of which attracted enormous adverse media publicity, Tatchell lost the by-election in February 1983, in a seat that was considered to be very 'safe' for Labour. No doubt the publicity had an enormously detrimental effect on Labour's fortunes in the general election of that year.

The Miners' Strike of 1984-85 represented an opportunity for the Labour Party to support a group of workers who were in the forefront of the struggle against the industrial policies of Margaret Thatcher's government. Support from the party leadership was lukewarm at best and, at times, seemed non-existent. The defeat of the strike and the bitter recriminations within the labour movement after it were, at the very least, largely the responsibility of the failure of Kinnock et al and, importantly, the leadership of the trade union movement, to wholeheartedly support the miners.

Kinnock's opportunistic abandonment, after the 1987 election and under pressure from the media, of his long-held support for unilateral nuclear disarmament, is also a good example in that it represented a complete reversal of his former position, not even in favour of multilateralism but instead for retaining Britain's 'nuclear capability'. Rather than attempting to argue the moral case for unilateralism, which he had supported for many years, Kinnock simply capitulated to media pressure.

The penultimate, and contemporary, example examined here is that of the 'news management' or 'spin-doctoring' initiated by Mandelson in 1985 and now under the control of Alastair Campbell. This represents the final achievement of the domination of image over substance. Given that Labour started life without any real specification of the content of its politics, it is hardly surprising that it achieved tremendous electoral success ninety-seven years later by emphasizing the form rather than the content. Only a party with a vacuum at its centre can do this, precisely because is has no guiding principles. Thus Labour's leaders are mostly presented as extremely able technocrats who are wrestling with the economic, social and political problems of the day. Rather than attempting to hegemonize or even challenge, New Labour is actually a response to the demands of the media, during the 1980s and 1990s, on behalf of so-called 'public opinion'.

We are now witnessing the return of the agreements with the Liberals that were initiated by MacDonald and Hardie all those years ago, although Charles Kennedy's succession to the leadership of the Liberal Democrats has somewhat tempered this process. Right throughout the party's history there are numerous examples of various types of co-oper-ation between the two parties, not least the 'Lib-Lab pact' of 1977-79. However, at the time Blair and Ashdown's alliance, which started in July 1997, just two months after the election, appeared to represent the successful resolution of a process that had started ninety-seven years earlier. It remains to be seen what will happen under the new Liberal Democrat leadership. Blair's hope is that the next century might belong to 'the radicals'. This could be said to be Hardie and MacDonald's project, but 101 years later!

What Labourism Is

This pact with the Liberals takes us right back to the beginning of the story, both historically and as regards the characterization of labourism being presented here. In one sense nothing has changed: the Labour government despite its huge parliamentary majority is seeking political co-operation with the Liberals. In 1900 and 1903 this might have been justified on pragmatic or electoral grounds, but this is certainly not the case in the late 1990s and early twenty-first century. Labour's majority of 175 seats in the House of Commons is unassailable. However, the economic, social and political landscape of Britain has been transformed almost beyond recognition in those 101 years. Industries that were the economic backbone of the country have grown, developed and died. The economy experienced severe depression in the 1930s, boom after the Second World War until the 1970s, depression and mass unemployment again in the 1980s and possibly something of a slight renaissance, mainly based on the services sector, in the 1990s. It is these changes that the Labour Party, in opposition and in government, has responded to by such things as the adoption of Keynesianism and, currently, neo-liberal economic policies. There is, then, also a sense in which everything has changed. The saying 'everything changes while everything stays the same' seems appropriate here. There have been huge and important changes to the party and trade unions during the last 101 years, many of which have been referred to in the text. A Labourite from the beginning of the century would, no doubt, find the party conference of the early twenty-first century a confusing place to be. However, in a very important sense, the boundaries of labourism have remained completely intact and have even been developed, particularly between 1945 and 1951 and in the late 1960s. They have experienced attacks and possibly even been slightly eroded at times, particularly by Gaitskell's revisionism and now Blair's New Labour. However, labourism is still alive and well in Britain in the early twenty-first century. If John Smith had not died in 1994 and had gone on to become Prime Minister, labourism would be even healthier, for the brief interregnum of Smith's leadership from 1992-94 represented a return to a more traditional approach than that of Kinnock before him and Blair after. The latter has constantly acknowledged his debt to John Smith (who had appointed him Shadow Home Secretary in 1992) and is not about to depart completely from the Smith legacy, despite constant rumours of the creation of a 'centre' party, breaking the link with the unions, and the possibility of state funding of political parties.

Many of the characteristics presented above overlap and are fundamentally inter-connected. The vague aim of social justice, the concentration on image over content that is based on an emotional rather than rational appeal, and the culture of defeatism are examples of this. The aim of social justice can be, and has been, presented in a very emotive and irrational manner and cannot achieve success precisely because it is so vague and undefined. All practice needs an element of theory no matter how unfocused and imprecise. To attempt to practice political activity on a supposedly pragmatic basis without reference to any theory is almost certainly going to lead to failure. In fact, it is this very issue that is central to the definition of labourism being presented in this book. Thus defeat is built into the very modus operandi of labourism.

It is right and proper that these characteristics overlap. They are not seven different aspects of the party and movement. Instead they are intended to add up to a notion of the phenomenon which can explain its failures and, very importantly, give rise to ideas regarding possible alternatives. If the absence of a clear ideology, vagueness of purpose, a contradictory view of representation, a misleading emotional appeal, lack of democracy, over-bureaucratization and a culture of defeatism are presented as criticisms, then obviously their converse are seen as positive features. Thus, a clear, unambiguous ideology and set of aims, a sound and consistent notion of representation, an emotional appeal based on actuality rather than deception, a thorough democratic accountability and decision-making process and a positive, proactive outlook are all essential prerequisites for a political party of the left.

For the whole of its existence the Labour Party has been committed to the ideal described in its 1929 manifesto, '…making Britain a happier and more contented land, and establishing peace in the world'. Without even beginning to attempt to articulate how they might go about achieving these highly ambitious and very laudable aims. Only infrequently has the party made any reference to the desirability, or otherwise, of the capitalist system. Much rhetoric appears to be based upon the premise that it is possible to wish the evils of capitalism away, while direct and unequivocal support is given to free market economics! Labourism is essentially a defensive response to some of the worst excesses of the capitalist system. Like trade unionism, out of which it grew, it actually needs capitalism in order to survive. Its very successes depend upon the successes of capitalism, as can be seen in the case study. It could almost be described as a parasitic growth on the capitalist system.

At a local level, labourism has meant a great deal to people struggling to make ends meet and has performed an extremely important symbolic task. It has been, as Miliband points out, no less than 'a way of life'. However, with the greatest possible respect to localities, the fact is that the power within labourism has always been concentrated at the national level of the party and movement and usually with the leader himself. Successive Labour leaders have wielded an enormous amount of power within the movement. Therefore, these concluding comments make no apology for the concentration in this book on the various pronouncements of Labour leaders, for it is they that have held the power, have made the important decisions and therefore are the main subjects of this characterization of labourism.

This survey of labourism has been necessarily wide-ranging and as a result perhaps slightly more superficial than might be thought desirable. It has attempted to encompass the whole of the party's thoughts and activities throughout its history and may therefore have lost some of the clarity of analysis that attention to detail can provide. However, the complexities of labourism have been examined and indicate that a one-line definition is neither possible nor desirable. The seven characteristics provided add up to a characterization.

A final brief mention should be made of the enduring influence of Fabianism. The Fabian Society, despite its initial lukewarm support for the LRC in 1900, has been the one organisation that has persisted right throughout the whole period. Its influence has hardly ever been very high-profile yet it has been consistent and important. A number of the characteristics of labourism can also be applied to the ideology and political practice of Fabianism, so perhaps its influence is greater than might at first appear. Perhaps it would be appropriate to view it as the labour movement equivalent of freemasonry. It continues to be very important within New Labour, not so much as an active think-tank in the way that Demos, Progress, Nexus and the IPPR are, but rather in the overall influence that Fabianism has had on the thinking of New Labour.

Characteristics of the nature of lack of ideology, vagueness, contradiction and defeatism do not add up to a positive view of labourism. Indeed, it becomes apparent why there is no widespread use of the term. The view of labourism presented here can be summarized, or visualized, as a structure with very strong boundaries, some of which were present in 1900 and some of which have been developed since then, but, unfortunately, with very little actual enduring content. Like many things, labourism has changed and yet it has remained the same. This book has concentrated upon the consistencies rather than the cleavages for one very important reason. While the different manifestations that the party has taken over the last 101 years are very significant, they nevertheless have all had essentially very similar effects on the economy, society and polity of Britain. It has been shown that there are many similarities as regards the vague aims and language of the founders of the party and those of its current leaders. Concepts of community, social justice, citizenship etc. are all to be found in the speeches and documents of both. This is no accident and these elements can be observed throughout the party's history. It would be foolish to suggest that there are no differences between the parties of MacDonald, Attlee, Gaitskell, Wilson, Kinnock and Blair. The aim here has been to show that however great these differences have been, they all represent different versions of the same overall approach to the political management of the British economy and society. It is this overall approach that this book has characterized as labourism.

Bibliography

Paul Adelman, *The Rise of the Labour Party 1880-1945*, Longman, London, 1972

Paul Anderson and Nyta Mann, *Safety First, The Making of New Labour*, Granta Books, London, 1997

Perry Anderson & Patrick Camiller (eds.), *Mapping the West European Left*, Verso, London, 1994

K.C. Barraclough, *Sheffield Steel*, Moorland Publishing, Buxton, 1976

Michael Barrat-Brown, *From Labourism to Socialism, The Political Economy of Labour in the 1970's*, Spokesman Books, Nottingham, 1972

Derek Bayliss (ed.) *A Guide to the Industrial History of South Yorkshire*, Association for Industrial Archaeology, Sheffield, 1995

Simon Beaufoy, *The Full Monty*, ScreenPress Books, Eye Suffolk, 1997

Geoffrey Beattie, *Survivors of Steel City, A Portrait of Sheffield*, Chatto and Windus, London, 1986

D.S. Bell & Byron Criddle, *The French Socialist Party, The Emergence of a Party of Government*, (second edition), Clarendon Press, Oxford, 1988

David S. Bell & Eric Shaw (eds.), *Conflict and Cohesion in Western European Social Democratic Parties*, Pinter, London & New York, 1994

R. Benewick, *Knowledge and Belief in Politics*, Allen and Unwin, London, 1973

Tony Benn, *Arguments for Socialism*, Penguin, Harmondsworth, 1980

Stefan Berger, *The British Labour Party and the German Social Democrats 1900-1931*, Clarendon Press, Oxford, 1994

Eduard Bernstein, *Evolutionary Socialism, A Criticism and Affirmation*, Schocken Books, New York, 1961

Clyde Binfield, Richard Childs, Roger Harper, David Hey, David Martin & Geoffrey Tweedale (eds.), *The History of the City of Sheffield, 1843-1993, Politics*, Sheffield Academic Press, 1993

Tony Blair, *Let Us Face the Future – the 1945 anniversary lecture*, Fabian Pamphlet 571, Fabian Society, London, 1995

Tony Blair, *New Britain, My Vision of a Young Country*, Fourth Estate, London, 1996

Tony Blair, *Socialism*, Fabian pamphlet 565, 1994

David Blunkett & Geoff Green, *Building from the Bottom, The Sheffield Experience*, Fabian Society, London, 1983

David Blunkett and Keith Jackson, *Democracy in Crisis, The Town Halls Respond*, Hogarth, London, 1987

Carl F. Brand, *The British Labour Party, A Short History*, revised edition, Stanford University Press, 1974

Brian Brivati and Tim Bale (eds.), *New Labour in Power, Precedents and prospects*,

Routledge, London, 1997

K.D. Brown (ed.), *The First Labour Party 1906-1914*, Croom Helm, London, 1985

David Butler and Dennis Kavanagh, *The British General Election of 1983*, Macmillan, London, 1984

Robert G. Burgess, *In the Field, An Introduction to Field Research*, Allen & Unwin, London, 1984

David Coates, *The Context of British Politics*, Hutchinson, London, 1984

David Coates, *The Crisis of Labour, Industrial Relations and the State in Contemporary Britain*, Philip Allan, Oxford, 1989

David Coates, *Labour Governments: Old Constraints and New Parameters* in *New Left Review*, No. 219, Sept/Oct 1996

David Coates, *The Labour Party and the Struggle for Socialism*, Cambridge University Press, 1975

David Coates, *Labour in Power? A Study of the Labour Government 1974-1979*, Longman, London, 1980

Ken Coates, *New Labour's Aims and Values, A Study in Ambiguity*, Socialist Renewal, European Labour Forum, Pamphlet no 3

George A. Codding, Jr. & William Safran, *Ideology and Politics: The Socialist Party of France*, Westview Press, Boulder, Colorado, 1979

G.D.H. Cole, *A History of the Labour Party from 1914*, Routledge & Kegan Paul, London 1948

F.W.S. Craig (ed.), *British General Election Manifestos 1900-1974*, Macmillan, London, 1975

F.W.S. Craig (ed.), *British General Election Manifestos 1959-1987*, Gower Books, Brookfield, Vermont, 1990

Anthony Crosland, *Social Democracy in Europe*, Fabian tract 438, Fabian Society, London, 1975

Radhika Desai, *Intellectuals and Socialism 'Social Democrats' and the Labour Party*, Lawrence & Wishart, London, 1994

Gregory Elliott, *Labourism and the English Genius, The Strange Death of Labour England?*, Verso, London, 1993

Steven Fielding, *The Labour Party, 'Socialism' and society since 1951*, Manchester University Press, 1997

Geoffrey Foote, *The Labour Party's Political Thought, A History*, Third Edition, Macmillan, Basingstoke, 1997

William Foote Whyte, *Learning from the Field, A Guide from Experience*, Sage Publications, Beverly Hills, 1984

Tom Forester, *The Labour Party and the Working Class*, Heinemann Educational, London, 1976

Anthony Giddens, *The Third Way, The Renewal of Social Democracy*, Polity, Cambridge, 1998

Richard Gillespie, *The Spanish Socialist Party, A History of Factionalism*, Clarendon Press, Oxford, 1989

Ian Gilmour, *Inside Right, A Study of Conservatism*, Hutchinson, London, 1977

Barney G. Glaser and Anselm L. Strauss, *The Discovery of Grounded Theory, Strategies for Qualitative Research*, Weidenfeld and Nicolson, London, 1967

W.L. Guttsman, *The German Social Democratic Party, 1875-1933*, From Ghetto to Government, George Allen & Unwin, London, 1981

Stuart Hall, *The Hard Road to Renewal, Thatcherism and the Crisis of the Left*, Verso, London, 1988

William Hampton, *Democracy and Community, A Study of Politics in Sheffield*, Oxford University Press, London, 1970

M. Donald Hancock et al, *Politics in Western Europe*, Macmillan, Basingstoke, 1993Kenneth Harris, *Attlee*, Weidenfeld and Nicolson, London, 1982

Stephen Haseler, *The Tragedy of Labour*, Blackwell, Oxford, 1980

Denis Healey, *The Time of My Life*, Penguin, London, 1989

Richard Heffernan and Mike Marqusee, *Defeat from the Jaws of Victory, Inside Kinnock's Labour Party*, Verso, London, 1992

Peter Hennessy & Anthony Seldon (eds.) *Ruling Performance, British Governments from Attlee to Thatcher*, Blackwell, Oxford, 1987

James Hinton, *Labour and Socialism, A History of the British Labour Movement 1867-1974*, Wheatsheaf Books, Brighton, 1983

Eric Hobsbawm (ed.), *The Forward March of Labour Halted?*, Verso, London, 1981

David Howell, *British Social Democracy, A Study in Development and Decay*, Croom Helm, London, 1980

HyperTribes Public Art Catalogue, Multimedia art in Sheffield City Centre 16 March – 25 April 1998

Kevin Jefferys, *The Labour Party Since 1945*, Macmillan, Basingstoke, 1993

Bill Jones (ed.), Andrew Gray, Dennis Kavanagh, Michael Moran, Philip Norton, Anthony Seldon, *Politics UK*, 3rd Edition, Prentice Hall Europe, Hemel Hempstead, 1998

Tudor Jones, *Remaking the Labour Party, From Gaitskell to Blair*, Routledge, London, 1996

Peter J. Katzenstein (ed.) *Industry and Politics in West Germany, Towards the Third Republic*, Cornell University Press, Ithaca, 1989

Colin Leys, *Politics in Britain, From Labourism to Thatcherism*, Verso, London, 1989

Labour into power: a framework for partnership, The Labour Party, London, January 1997

The Labour Party conference verbatim report, 30 Sept.-4 Oct. 1996, Labour Party, London, 1996

The Labour Party Foundation Conference and Annual Conference Reports 1900-1905, Hammersmith Bookshop Ltd, London, 1967

George Lichtheim, *A Short History of Socialism*, Fontana, London, 1970

Peter Mandelson and Roger Liddle, *The Blair Revolution, Can New Labour Deliver?*, Faber and Faber, London, 1996

David Marquand, *The Progressive Dilemma*, Heinemann, London, 1992

John Marriott, *The Culture of Labourism, The East End Between the Wars*, Edinburgh University Press, 1991

A.M. McBriar, *Fabian Socialism and English Politics 1884-1918*, Cambridge University Press, 1966

Robert McKenzie, *British Political Parties, The Distribution of Power within the Conservative and Labour Parties*, (Second Edition), Heinemann, London, 1963

Ross McKibbin, *The Evolution of the Labour Party 1910-1924*, Oxford University Press, 1974

Ross McKibbin, *The Ideologies of Class, Social Relations in Britain 1880-1950*, Clarendon Press, Oxford, 1990

David McLellan, *Ideology*, Open University Press, Buckingham, 1995

Andy McSmith, *Faces of Labour, The Inside Story*, Verso, London, 1996

Robert Michels, *Political Parties, A Sociological Study of the Oligarchical Tendencies of Modern Democracy*, Free Press, New York, 1962

Ralph Miliband, *Marxism and Politics*, Oxford University Press, Oxford, 1977

Ralph Miliband, *Parliamentary Socialism, A Study in the Politics of Labour*, Merlin Press, London, 1972

Susanne Miller and Heinrich Potthoff, *A History of German Social Democracy, From 1848 to the Present*, Berg, Leamington Spa, 1986

Lewis Minkin, *The Contentious Alliance. Trade Unions and the Labour Party*, Edinburgh University Press, 1991

Lewis Minkin, *The Labour Party Conference*, Allen Lane, London, 1978

Roger Moore, *The Emergence of the Labour Party 1880-1924*, Hodder and Stoughton, London, 1978

New Labour: Because Britain Deserves Better, 1997 election manifesto, The Labour Party, 1997

Kenneth O. Morgan, *Labour in Power 1945-1951*, Oxford University Press, 1984

Tom Nairn, *The nature of the Labour Party-1 & 2* in *New Left Review*, No's 27 & 28, Sept/Oct, Nov/Dec, 1964

The New Hope for Britain, Labour's Manifesto 1983, Labour Party, London, 1983

New Labour and the Labour Movement, Conference Proceedings, University of Sheffield, June 1998

Stephen Padgett & William E. Paterson, *A History of Social Democracy in Postwar Europe*, Longman, Harlow, 1991.

Leo Panitch and Colin Leys, *The End of Parliamentary Socialism, From New Left to New Labour*, Verso, London, 1997

Leo Panitch, *Social Democracy and Industrial Militancy, The Labour Party, the Trade Unions and Incomes Policy, 1945-1974*, Cambridge University Press, 1976

Leo Panitch, *Working-Class Politics in Crisis, Essays on Labour and the State*, Verso, London, 1986

Partnership in Power, The Labour Party, London, 1997

Diane L. Parness, *The SPD and the Challenge of Mass Politics, The Dilemma of the German Volkspartei*, Westview, Boulder, Colorado, 1991

William E. Paterson and Alastair H. Thomas (eds.) *The Future of Social Democracy, Problems and Prospects of Social Democratic Parties in Western Europe*, Clarendon Press, Oxford, 1986

William E. Paterson & Alastair H. Thomas (eds.), *Social Democratic Parties in Western Europe*, Croom Helm, London, 1977

Edward R. Pease, *The History of the Fabian Society*, Cass, London, 1963

Henry Pelling, *The Origins of the Labour Party 1880-1900*, Clarendon Press, Oxford, 1965

Henry Pelling, *A Short History of the Labour Party*, 10th edition, Macmillan Press,

Basingstoke, 1993

Gordon Phillips, *The Rise of the Labour Party 1893-1931*, Routledge, London, 1992

Sidney Pollard, *A History of Labour in Sheffield*, Liverpool University Press, 1959

Jonas Pontusson, *Swedish Social Democracy and British Labour: Essays on the Nature and Conditions of Social Democratic Hegemony*, Cornell University, 1988

Programme of the Swedish Social Democratic Party, adopted by the 1975 Party Congress, Social Democratic Party of Sweden, 1975

Adam Przeworski, *Capitalism and social democracy*, Cambridge University Press, Cambridge, 1985

Adam Przeworski & John Sprague, *Paper Stones, A History of Electoral Socialism*, University of Chicago Press, Chicago, 1986

Report of the Sixth Annual Conference of the Labour Party, Labour Party, London, 1906

Report of the 44th Annual Conference, Labour Party, London, 1945

Report of the Annual Conference of the Labour Party 1983, Labour Party, London, 1983

Theodore Rothstein, *From Chartism to Labourism, Historical Sketches of the English Working Class Movement*, Martin Lawrence, London, 1929

Raphael Samuel and Gareth Stedman Jones (eds.), *Culture, Ideology and Politics, Essays for Eric Hobsbawm*, Routledge & Kegan Paul, London, 1982

Donald Sassoon, *Social Democracy at the Heart of Europe*, IPPR, London, 1996

John Saville, *The Ideology of Labourism* in R. Benewick, *Knowledge and Belief in Politics*, Allen and Unwin, London, 1973

John Saville, *The Labour Movement in Britain, A Commentary*, Faber and Faber, London, 1988

Fritz W. Scharpf, *Crisis and Choice in European Social Democracy*, Cornell University Press, Ithaca & London, 1991

Carl E. Schorske, *German Social Democracy, 1905-1917, The Development of the Great Schism*, Harvard University Press, Cambridge Massachusetts, 1983

Patrick Seyd, *The Political Management of Decline 1973-1993* in Binfield, Childs, Harper, Hey, Martin & Tweedale (eds.) *The History of the City of Sheffield, Politics*, Sheffield Academic Press, 1993

Eric Shaw, *The Labour Party since 1945, Old Labour: New Labour*, Blackwell, Oxford, 1996

Sheffield City Council, Housing & Direct Services, *Cross Talk, The Parson Cross Newsletter*, July 1998

Sheffield, The Second Slump, A Draft Report for Sheffield Trades Council, 1982

Philip Snowden, *What is the Labour Party? A reply to Liberal Misrepresentations*, 1922?

Peter Tatchell, *The Battle for Bermondsey*, Heretic Books, London, 1983

Andrew J. Taylor, *The Trade Unions and the Labour Party*, Croom Helm, London, 1987

Ian Taylor, Karen Evans and Penny Fraser, *A Tale of Two Cities, Global change, local feeling and everyday life in the North of England. A Study in Manchester and Sheffield*, Routledge, London, 1996

Willie Thompson, *The Long Death of British Labourism: Interpreting a Political Culture*, Pluto Press, London, 1993

Andrew Thorpe, *A History of the British Labour Party*, Macmillan, Basingstoke, 1997

Tim Tilton, *The Political Theory of Swedish Social Democracy, Through the Welfare State to Socialism*, Clarendon Press, Oxford, 1991

Roy Turner (ed.), *Ethnomethodology, Selected Readings*, Penguin Educational, Harmondsworth, 1974

Martin Upham, *Tempered – Not Quenched, The History of the ISTC 1951-1997*, Lawrence and Wishart, London, 1997

Hilary Wainwright, *Arguments for a New Left, Answering the Free-Market Right*, Blackwell, Oxford, 1994

Hilary Wainwright, *Labour, A Tale of Two Parties*, Hogarth, London, 1987

Hilary Wainwright, 'Once More Moving On: Social Movements, Political Representation and the Future of the Radical Left' in Panitch (ed.) *Socialist Register 1995*, Merlin, 1995

Paul Whiteley, *The Labour Party in Crisis*, Methuen, London, 1983

Stuart Williams (ed.), *Socialism in France, From Jaures to Mitterand*, St. Martin's Press, New York, 1983.

Tony Wright, *Who Wins Dares, New Labour – New Politics*, Fabian Society, London, 1997

Yorkshire & Humberside Steel Strike Committee, *Steel Steel Steel Steel Steel Strike!, An illustrated review*

References

1   Peter Hennessy & Anthony Seldon (eds.) *Ruling Performance,British Governments from Attlee to Thatcher*, Blackwell, Oxford, 1987, p. 188

2   Geoffrey Foote is a Senior Lecturer in History at the University of Teeside and Thomas Hodgskin was a dominant figure in the free labour movement of the early part of the 19th century.

3   Geoffrey Foote, *The Labour Party's Political Thought, A History*, Third Edition, Macmillan, Basingstoke, 1997, p. 5

4   Ibid., p. 12

5   Theodore Rothstein was born in Russia in 1871. He worked in England as a journalist between 1891 and 1920, when he returned to Russia. He was a member of the Social Democratic Federation and later the British Socialist Party.

6   Theodore Rothstein, *From Chartism to Labourism, Historical Sketches of the English Working Class Movement*, Martin Lawrence, London, 1929, p. 7

7   Theodore Rothstein, *From Chartism to Labourism, Historical Sketches of the English Working Class Movement*, Martin Lawrence, London, 1929, p. 284

8   Ibid, p. 297

9   Ibid, p. 318

10   Ralph Miliband was Professor of Politics at Leeds University and co-editor of *Socialist Register*. He died in 1994

11   Ralph Miliband, *Parliamentary Socialism, A Study in the Politics of Labour*, Second Edition, Merlin Press, London, 1972, p. 61

12   Ibid., p. 13

13   Geoffrey Foote, *The Labour Party's Political Thought, A History*, Third Edition, Macmillan, Basingstoke, 1997, pp. 7, 8

14   Ralph Miliband, *Parliamentary Socialism, A Study in the Politics of Labour*, Second Edition, Merlin Press, London, 1972, p. 17

15   Ibid., p. 144

16   Ibid., p. 104

17   *The Independent*, 11.9.1996

18   *The Guardian*, 1.3.1997

19   Lewis Minkin, *The Contentious Alliance, Trade Unions and the Labour Party*, Edinburgh University Press, 1991, p. 3

20   Ralph Miliband, *Parliamentary Socialism, A Study in the Politics of Labour*, Second Edition, Merlin Press, London, 1972, p. 16

21   John Saville is Emeritus Professor of Economic History at the University of

Hull.

22　John Saville, *The Ideology of Labourism* in R. Benewick, *Knowledge and Belief in Politics*, Allen and Unwin, London, 1973, pp. 215, 216

23　John Saville, *The Labour Movement in Britain, A Commentary*, Faber & Faber, London, 1988, p. 21

24　David Coates was Professor of Government at the University of Manchester and is currently Worrell Professor of Anglo-American Studies at Wake Forest University, North Carolina.

25　David Coates, *Labour in Power? A Study of the Labour Government 1974-1979*, Longman, London, 1980, p. 271

26　David Coates, *The Crisis of Labour, Industrial Relations and the State in Contemporary Britain*, Philip Allan, Oxford, 1989, p. 36

27　Tom Nairn is Scottish and was an editor of *New Left Review*.

28　Tom Nairn, *The nature of the Labour Party-1* in *New Left Review*, No 27, Sept/Oct, 1964, p. 44

29　Ibid., p. 45

30　Ibid., p. 45

31　Tom Nairn, *The nature of the Labour Party – 2* in *New Left* Review, No 28, Nov/Dec, 1964, p. 62

32　Tom Forester was a journalist for *New Society, The Times, The Guardian* and *New Statesman*.

33　Tom Forester, *The Labour Party and the Working Class*, Heinemann, London, 1976, p. 31

34　Stephen Haseler was Professor of Government at City of London Polytechnic and is Chair of *Republic*

35　Stephen Haseler, *The Tragedy of Labour*, Blackwell, Oxford, 1980, p. 14

36　John Marriott, *The Culture of Labourism, The East End Between the Wars*, Edinburgh University Press, 1991, p. 9

37　Ibid., p. 12

38　Ibid., p. 163

39　Willie Thompson teaches history at Glasgow Caledonian University and is the editor of *Socialist History*.

40　Willie Thompson, *The Long Death of British Labourism, Interpreting a Political Culture*, Pluto Press, London, 1993, p. 6

41　Ibid., p. 6

42　Gregory Elliott is a member of the editorial collective of *Radical Philosophy*.

43　Gregory Elliott, *Labourism and the English Genius, The Strange Death of Labour England?*, Verso, London, 1993, p. xiii

44　Radhika Desai teaches politics at the University of Victoria, Canada.

45　Radhika Desai, *Intellectuals and Socialism, 'Social Democrats' and the Labour Party*, Lawrence & Wishart, London, 1994, p. 6

46　Ibid., p. 102

47　Michael Barrat Brown is a long-standing member of the Labour Party and writes extensively for the Socialist Renewal group. Colin Leys is Emeritus Professor at Queen's University, Canada and co-editor of *Socialist Register*.

48　Colin Leys, *Politics in Britain, From Labourism to Thatcherism*, Revised Edition,

Verso, London, 1989, p. 215

49   Ibid., p. 229
50   Ibid., p. 232
51   Hilary Wainwright is editor of *Red Pepper* and a long-time leading member of various independent left organisations.
52   Hilary Wainwright, *Labour: A Tale of Two Parties*, Hogarth, London, 1987, p. 14
53   Hilary Wainwright, *Arguments for a New Left, Answering the Free Market Right*, Blackwell, Oxford, 1994, pp. 205, 206
54   Leo Panitch, *Social Democracy and Industrial Militancy, The Labour Party, the Trade Unions and Incomes Policy, 1945-1974*, Cambridge University Press, 1976, p. 1
55   Leo Panitch, *Working-Class Politics in Crisis, Essays on Labour and the State*, Verso, London, 1986, p. 5
56   Leo Panitch & Colin Leys, *The End of Parliamentary Socialism, From New Left to New Labour*, Verso, London, 1997, p. vii
57   Stuart Hall, *The Hard Road to Renewal, Thatcherism and the Crisis of the Left*, Verso, London, 1988, p. 51
58   Ibid., p. 183
59   As already mentioned in relation to Miliband, this book does not agree with this notion.
60   *The Concise Oxford Dictionary*, Ninth Edition, Clarendon Press, Oxford, 1995
61   Henry Pelling, *The Origins of the Labour Party 1880-1900*, Macmillan, London, 1965, p. 118
62   Ibid., p. 118
63   Ibid., p. 33
64   Ibid., p. 34
65   Edward R. Pease, *The History of the Fabian Society*, Cass, London, 1963 , p. 37
66   *Oxford English Dictionary*, 2nd edition, Clarendon Press, Oxford, 1989
67   Edward R. Pease, *The History of the Fabian Society*, Cass, London, 1963, p. 39
68   Henry Pelling, *The Origins of the Labour Party 1880-1900*, Macmillan, London, 1965, p. 35
69   Paul Adelman, *The Rise of the Labour Party 1880-1945*, Longman, London, 1972, p. 9
70   Henry Pelling, *The Origins of the Labour Party 1880-1900*, Macmillan, London, 1965, pp. 204, 205
71   Paul Adelman, *The Rise of the Labour Party 1880-1945*, Longman, London, 1972, p. 16
72   Henry Pelling, *A Short History of the Labour Party*, Macmillan, London, 1982, p. 7
73   Henry Pelling, *The Origins of the Labour Party 1880-1900*, Macmillan, London, 1965, p. 206
74   *The Labour Party Foundation Conference and Annual Conference Reports 1900-1905*, Hammersmith Bookshop Ltd, London, 1967, p. 12
75   Ibid., p. 17
76   Ibid., p. 11
77   Ibid., p. 17
78   Ibid., p. 17

79   F.W.S. Craig (ed.), *British General Election Manifestos 1900-1974*, Macmillan, London, 1975, p. 4

80   F.W.S. Craig(ed.), *British General Election Manifestos 1900-1974*, Macmillan, London, 1975, p. 20

81   Ross McKibbin, *The Evolution of the Labour Party, 1910-1924*, Oxford University Press, 1974, p. xv

82   Ibid., p. xvi

83   K.D. Brown (ed.), *The First Labour Party 1906-1914*, Croom Helm, London, 1985, p. 4

84   *The Labour Party Foundation Conference and Annual Conference Reports 1900-1905*, Hammersmith Bookshop Ltd, London, 1967, p. 45

85   K.D. Brown(ed.), *The First Labour Party 1906-1914*, Croom Helm, London, 1985, p. 7

86   Ibid., p. 9

87   Ibid., pp. 31, 32

88   Ralph Miliband, *Parliamentary Socialism, A Study in the Politics of Labour*, Second Edition, Merlin Press, London, 1972, p. 28

89   Henry Pelling, *A Short History of the Labour Party*, Macmillan, London, 1993, p. 25

90   Ralph Miliband, *Parliamentary Socialism, A Study in the Politics of Labour*, Second Edition, Merlin Press, London, 1972, p. 29

91   K.D. Brown(ed.), *The First Labour Party 1906-1914*, Croom Helm, London, 1985, p. 1

92   Ross McKibbin, *The Evolution of the Labour Party, 1910-1924*, Oxford University Press, 1974, p. 1

93   Paul Adelman, *The Rise of the Labour Party 1880-1945*, Longman, London, 1972, p. 50

94   G.D.H. Cole, *A History of the Labour Party from 1914*, Routledge & Kegan Paul, London, 1948, p. 72

95   Tony Benn, *Arguments for Socialism*, Penguin, Harmondsworth, 1980. p. 39

96   Ken Coates, *New Labour's Aims and Values, A Study in Ambiguity*, Spokesman, Nottingham, p. 1

97   Tony Blair, *Let Us Face the Future-the 1945 anniversary lecture*, Fabian Pamphlet 571, Fabian Society, London, 1995, p. 12

98   Ross McKibbin, *The Evolution of the Labour Party 1910-1924*, Oxford University Press, 1974, pp. 96, 97

99   Ibid., p. 97

100   Ibid., p. 244

101   G.D.H. Cole, *A History of the Labour Party from 1914*, Routledge & Kegan Paul, London, 1948, p. 54

102   Ralph Miliband, *Parliamentary Socialism, A Study in the Politics of Labour*, Second Edition, Merlin Press, London, 1972, p. 62

103   Ross McKibbin, *The Evolution of the Labour Party 1910-1924*, Oxford University Press, 1974, p. 245

104   Ibid., p. 247

105   Ralph Miliband, *Parliamentary Socialism, A Study in the Politics of Labour*,

Second Edition, Merlin Press, London, 1972, p. 100

106 Ibid., p. 100

107 Ibid., p. 101

108 Ibid., p. 144

109 *Report of the 44th Annual Conference*, Labour Party , London, 1945, p. 90

110 Ibid., pp. 95, 96

111 F.W.S. Craig (ed.), *British General Election Manifestos 1900-1974*, Macmillan, London, 1975, p. 124

112 Ibid., p. 127

113 Ralph Miliband, *Parliamentary Socialism, A Study in the Politics of Labour*, Second Edition, Merlin Press, London, 1972, p. 280

114 Ibid., p. 279

115 Ibid., p. 345

116 David Coates, *The Labour Party and the Struggle for Socialism*, Cambridge University Press, 1975, pp. 98, 99

117 Ibid., p. 98

118 F.W.S. Craig (ed.), *British General Election Manifestos 1900-1974*, Macmillan, London, 1975, pp. 405, 406

119 Denis Healey, *The Time of My Life*, Penguin, London, 1989, p. 500

120 *The New Hope for Britain, Labour's Manifesto 1983*, Labour Party , London, 1983, p. 4

121 Tony Blair, *New Britain, My Vision of a Young Country*, Fourth Estate, London, 1996, p. 29

122 Tony Blair, *Let Us Face the Future-the 1945 anniversary lecture*, Fabian Pamphlet 571, Fabian Society, London, 1995, p. 14

123 Tony Blair, *New Britain, My Vision of a Young Country*, Fourth Estate, London, 1996, p. 18

124 Ibid., p. 18

125 Anthony Giddens, *The Third Way, The Renewal of Social Democracy*, Polity, Cambridge 1998

126 Tony Wright, *Who Wins Dares, New Labour – New Politics*, Fabian Society, London, 1997

127 Ken Coates, *New Labour's Aims and Values, A Study in Ambiguity*, Spokesman, Nottingham, p. 2

128 Ibid, p. 2

129 Sixteen people were interviewed in total. They are, in alphabetical order, with the labour movement positions they currently or most recently held: Roger Barton, MEP for Sheffield, Barnsley West and Penistone; Clive Betts, MP for Sheffield, Attercliffe and Assistant Government Whip; Peter Birch, Convenor, AEU; David Blunkett, MP for Sheffield, Brightside and Secretary of State for Education & Employment; Charlie Darville, Chair, Sheffield Pensioners Action Group; Terry Gardner, Branch Secretary, Stocksbridge Chemist's Branch, ISTC; Seaton Gosling, Chair, Black Community Forum; Pat Heath, Chair of Social Services, Sheffield City Council; Peter Horton, Chair of Education/Lord Mayor, Sheffield City Council; Helen Jackson, MP for Sheffield, Hillsborough and PPS to Secretary of State for NI; Alan Jones, Councillor , South Yorkshire County

Council; Bill Michie, MP for Sheffield, Heeley; Dan Sequerra, Director, Employment Department, Sheffield City Council; Mandy Siberry, Women's Officer/Education Officer for UNISON- Yorkshire and Humberside region; Ted Thorne, Branch Secretary, Templeborough Branch, ISTC; Alan Wigfield, Chair of Housing and Chief Whip, Sheffield City Council. Past positions held will be referred to in the text, as appropriate.

130 From *Sheffield, The Second Slump*, A Draft Report for Sheffield Trades Council, 1982

131 Ian Taylor, Karen Evans and Penny Fraser, *A Tale of Two Cities, Global change, local feeling and everyday life in the North of England. A study in Manchester and Sheffield*, Routledge, London, 1996, p. 40

132 From *Sheffield, The Second Slump*, A Draft Report for Sheffield Trades Council, 1982

133 From *Sheffield, The Second Slump*, A Draft Report for Sheffield Trades Council, 1982

134 David Blunkett & Geoff Green, *Building from the Bottom, The Sheffield Experience*, Fabian Society, London, 1983, p. 13

135 From Patrick Seyd, *The Political Management of Decline, 1973-1993* in Binfield et al *The History of the City of Sheffield 1843-1993, Politics*, Sheffield Academic Press, 1993

136 From Ian Taylor, Karen Evans and Penny Fraser, *A Tale of Two Cities, Global change, local feeling and everyday life in the North of England. A study in Manchester and Sheffield*, Croom Helm, London, 1996

137 From *The Guardian*, Monday, March 16, 1998

138 From Patrick Seyd, *The Political Management of Decline, 1973-1993* in Binfield et al *The History of the City of Sheffield 1843-1993, Politics*, Sheffield Academic Press, 1993.

139 From Patrick Seyd, *The Political Management of Decline, 1973-1993* in Binfield et al *The History of the City of Sheffield 1843-1993, Politics*, Sheffield Academic Press, 1993.

140 From *The Guardian*, Monday, March 16, 1998

141 From Ian Taylor, Karen Evans and Penny Fraser, *A Tale of Two Cities, Global change, local feeling and everyday life in the North of England. A study in Manchester and Sheffield*, Croom Helm, London, 1996.

142 From Patrick Seyd, *The Political Management of Decline, 1973-1993* in Binfield et al *The History of the City of Sheffield 1843-1993, Politics*, Sheffield Academic Press, 1993.

143 From Sheffield City Council, Electoral Services.

144 The de-selection of Eddie Griffiths, the ISTC sponsored MP for Brightside, and the selection of Joan Maynard, a left-winger, to fight and win the seat in the second general election of 1974.

145 David Blunkett & Geoff Green, *Building from the Bottom, The Sheffield Experience*, Fabian Society, London, 1983, p. 4

146 Ibid., p. 28

147 Patrick Seyd, *The Political Management of Decline 1973-1993* in Binfield et al *The History of the City of Sheffield, Politics*, Sheffield Academic Press, 1993

148 Patrick Seyd, *The Political Management of Decline 1973-1993* in Binfield et al *The History of the City of Sheffield, Politics*, Sheffield Academic Press, 1993, p. 168

149 Ibid., p. 184

150 From *The Guardian*, Monday, March 16, 1998

151 No enjoyment has been taken from the critique of a once proud, vibrant, effective and near-hegemonic movement. In fact, quite the opposite is the case. The personal, and therefore emotional, involvement with the subject matter has made dealing with the issues very difficult and sometimes even painful. The respect felt for the strong traditions and effectiveness of the local labour movement cannot be overstated. The *Sheffield* movement was therefore, for me, *the most difficult*, out of any in the whole country, to criticize.

152 Sheffield City Council, Housing & Direct Services, *Cross Talk, The Parson Cross Newsletter*, July 1998

153 From North East Sheffield Trust, *NEST Community Audit*, Spring 1997

154 *HyperTribes Public Art Catalogue*, Multimedia art in Sheffield City Centre 16 March – 25 April 1998, p. 7

155 *Sheffield, The Second Slump*, A Draft Report for Sheffield Trades Council, 1982

156 Many of the hopes I expressed in this chapter have been dashed, in the period since the case study was completed.

157 From *The Guardian* 8.5.1999, p. 4

158 The telling of these events gives me no pleasure whatsoever. In fact it fills me with dismay.

159 Ralph Miliband, *Parliamentary Socialism, A Study in the Politics of Labour*, 2nd edition, Merlin Press, London, 1972, p. 101

160 The Labour Party, *New Labour, because Britain deserves better*, election manifesto 1997, p. 4

161 Ian Gilmour, *Inside Right, A Study of Conservatism*, 1977, p. 109

162 *The Concise Oxford Dictionary*, 1995

163 Geoffrey Foote, *The Labour Party's Political Thought, A History*, 1997, p. 61

164 Ralph Miliband, *Parliamentary Socialism, A Study in the Politics of Labour*, 1972, p. 31

165 Tony Blair, *New Britain, My Vision of a Young Country*, 1996, pp. 38, 39

166 Philip Snowden, *What is the Labour Party? A Reply to Liberal Misrepresentations*, 1922[?], p. 2

167 Kenneth Harris, *Attlee*, Weidenfeld and Nicolson, London, 1982, p. 468

168 F.W.S. Craig (ed.) *British General Election Manifestos 1900-1974*, Macmillan, London, 1975, p. 208

169 Eric Shaw, *The Labour Party since 1945, Old Labour: New Labour*, Blackwell, Oxford, 1996, p. 54

170 David Coates, *Labour in Power? A Study of the Labour Government 1974-1979*, Longman, London, 1980, p. 5

171 Brian Brivati & Tim Bale, *New Labour in Power, precedents and prospects*, Routledge, London, 1997, pp. 51, 52

172 Tony Blair, *New Britain, My Vision of a Young Country*, Fourth Estate, London, 1996, p. 150

173   F.W.S. Craig (ed.) *British General Election Manifestos 1900-1974*, Macmillan, London, 1975, p. 4

174   Ross McKibbin, *The Evolution of the Labour Party, 1910-1924*, Oxford University Press, 1974, p. xvi

175   Ralph Miliband, *Parliamentary Socialism, A Study in the Politics of Labour*, Merlin Press, London, 1972, p. 19

176   *The Labour Party Foundation Conference and Annual Conference Reports 1900-1905*, Hammersmith Bookshop Ltd, London, 1967, p. 45

177   Ibid., p. 17

178   Lewis Minkin, *The Labour Party Conference, A Study in the Politics of Intra-Party Democracy*, Allen Lane, London, 1978, p. 7

179   Ibid., p. 9

180   Ibid., p. ix

181   Ibid., p. 13

182   Tony Blair, *New Britain, My Vision of a Young Country*, Fourth Estate, London, 1996, p. 4

183   Ibid., p. 18

184   Cited in David Coates, *Labour Governments: Old Constraints and New Parameters* in *New Left Review*, No. 219, Sept/Oct 1996, p. 74

185   Lewis Minkin, *The Labour Party Conference, A Study in the Politics of Intra-Party Democracy*, Allen Lane, London, 1978, p. 8

186   Lewis Minkin, *The Contentious Alliance, Trade Unions and the Labour Party*, Edinburgh University Press, 1991, p. 3

187   From ibid.

188   From *The Times*, 22.4.1998

189   From Leo Panitch & Colin Leys, *The End of Parliamentary Socialism, From New Left to New Labour*, Verso, London, 1997

190   From *The Times*, 22.4.1998

191   Geoffrey Foote, *The Labour Party's Political Thought, A History*, Third Edition, Macmillan, Basingstoke, 1997, p. 63

192   Kenneth Harris, *Attlee*, Weidenfeld and Nicolson, London, 1982, p. 257

193   David Coates, *The Labour Party and the Struggle for Socialism*, Cambridge University Press, 1975, p. 99

194   *The Labour Party conference verbatim report, 30 Sept-4 Oct. 1996*, Labour Party, London, 1996, p. 82

195   The Labour Party, *New Labour, because Britain deserves better*, election manifesto 1997, p. 2

196   David Marquand, *The Progressive Dilemma*, Heinemann, London, 1992, p. 207

197   Lewis Minkin, *The Contentious Alliance, Trade Unions and the Labour Party*, Edinburgh University Press, 1991, p. 5

198   Geoffrey Foote, *The Labour Party's Political Thought, A History*, Third Edition, Macmillan, Basingstoke, 1997, p. 48

199   David Coates, *The Labour Party and the Struggle for Socialism*, Cambridge University Press, 1975 p. 98

200   David Marquand, *The Progressive Dilemma*, Heinemann, London, 1992, p. 206

201   Richard Heffernan & Mike Marqusee, *Defeat from the Jaws of Victory, Inside*

Kinnock's Labour Party, Verso, London, 1992, pp. 105, 106

202 *The Labour Party conference verbatim report, 30 Sept – 4 Oct, 1996*, Labour Party, London, 1996, p. 80

203 Ross McKibbin, *The Evolution of the Labour Party 1910-1924*, Oxford University Press, 1974, p. 245

204 Lewis Minkin, *The Labour Party Conference, A Study in the Politics of Intra-Party Democracy*, Allen Lane, London, 1978, p. 6

205 Ibid., p. 9

206 The Labour Party, *Partnership in Power*, Labour Party, London, 1997, p. 7

207 Lewis Minkin, *The Labour Party Conference, A Study in the Politics of Intra-Party Democracy*, Allen Lane, London, 1978, p. 11

208 Robert McKenzie, *British Political Parties, The Distribution of Power within the Conservative and Labour* Parties, (Second Edition), Heinemann, London, 1963, p. 485

209 *New Labour and the Labour Movement*, Conference Proceedings, Political Economy Research Centre, University of Sheffield and International Centre for Labour Studies, University of Manchester, 1998, pp. 54, 55

210 The Labour Party, *Labour into power: a framework for partnership*, Labour Party, London, January 1997, pp. 13, 14

211 Ralph Miliband, *Parliamentary Socialism, A Study in the Politics of Labour*, Merlin Press, London, 1972, p. 144

Index